Every male has the drive to become a real man.

Other men guide him on this adventure.

A strong father invests in his son's manhood quest.

This book challenges courageous warriors on this God-intended journey.

BULL

Mitchell P. Davis, B.A.
Roy Smith, M.Div., Ph.D.

ISBN: 978-0-9842094-2-2

Book cover and interior design by Laura Cramer

Special Thanks
To These
Bull Elephants In My Life

Uncle Roy

Uncle Don

Uncle Paul

Uncle Tim

Uncle Ron

Chuck "Coach" Harrison

Shane Manney

Joel Hutchinson

Dr. T

Dr. Beck

And above all else, thanks
to my father for everything
he has done for me.

Contents

Foreword i

Introduction v

Manhood Discussion Instructions ix

1. Here Enter Boys To Become Men 1
2. Use Your Left Foot 8
3. One Warning, Two Cats 13
4. Go West, Young Man 19
5. Understanding That You Are Terrible With Numbers 24
6. Why Is It Important To Communicate? 28
7. The Bulls At Bloomsburg 36
8. Prove It, My Friend 42
9. All Things To All People 47
10. The Art Of Being Authentic 53
11. Make Me Proud, Become A Farmer 58
12. Boredom: A Man's Worst Enemy 62
13. Dehydration, Red Gatorade, And Gratitude 68
14. Some Ping Pong And Simon & Garfunkel 73
15. The Top Five Decisions That Determine A Man's Future (Part 1) 77
16. The Top Five Decisions That Determine A Man's Future (Part 2) 81
17. Balance, Cooperation, The Adventure, And Number 1 87
18. Private: Stay Out 96
19. War Horse 103
20. How Do We Decide What Is Right And Wrong? 108
21. What Does A Man Do When He Is Wrong? 114
22. When Good Bulls Go Bad 119
23. What Do We Do About God? 127
24. What Now? 141
25. The Talk 148

Father/Son Survey 151
The Bull Team 153

Foreword

To the Young Men

Welcome to the world of *Bull*. This book has been written to call you young males to step up and become men. There are not enough men in the world and because of this, the world is hurting. Girls need not apply, for the road ahead is not for females. We ask that you read 5-12 pages each week and answer some tough questions. Whether in an accountability group of other young males or on a journey with your dad or mentor, you will be challenged to look at life differently. The world teaches that males are simplistic, unable to feel, not real bright, aggressive, and also need to be told "No" a lot. We believe differently.

Those of us on the *Bull* team have a more positive view and we expect a lot. You are talented in ways that many are not. As a result, we need you to become a man, as well as part of our team. To do this, you must understand how you are made (your design), suck it up and develop yourself. The important issues of living life must be worked on. This will cause some sweat as you talk about certain subjects that you have never talked about before. Now, we are not God, so everything we say that we believe may not be right. We think it is. However, as a man, it is important and expected that you learn to think for yourself, which means, even if you agree with us, you must wrestle with the information that is presented until it becomes yours.

Any journey into manhood cannot be taken alone, so reading this by yourself is a start, but doing it with another person is the only way that manhood is developed. As two guys talk about how they live, both their similarities and differences will be understood. These discussions, which sharpen you, also create the sparks that ignite growth toward manhood. You must learn to express your disagreement, for it is important to share your opinions, sharpen your thoughts, and understand your manhood at deeper levels.

Males who read *Bull* will be from diverse backgrounds. Some will be living in different countries, with advantages and disadvantages with which you are unfamiliar. Life demands similar things, however, for a male to become a man. In this way, we are all expected to toughen up, make the right choices, develop strong relationships, fulfill our design, and be willing to fight for what is true. If you don't work to apply this adventure to your life in practical ways, all of what you are learning will have little or no effect on your journey; it will be like water rolling off a duck's back *(most countries have ducks)*. For some of you, talking to your father about what counts in life will be familiar and comfortable. For others, this level of intense conversation will be a challenging experience for you and for your dad (or mentor). Pace yourselves, stretch a little each time, and it will get easier. When a man works to solidify his manhood, it will be affirmed by the other men in his life. It can't be bought nor can it be stolen; it is not achieved by simply saying you are a man. So, choose your manhood team and get to work!

This book has been written for young males - teenagers or older. It is never too early or too late to start the manhood process. If you are a young male, read this book and use it as a resource to help you prepare for your teenage years. This is one of two books that will outline the manhood journey. The second one is called *Being God's Man*. Whether you just read one book or read both, you will benefit. We believe that the *Bible* is true, and that it teaches us about God and how to have a relationship with Him. Our spiritual viewpoint will be expressed clearly. What you do with it is up to you. What is not okay is for you to ignore the spiritual aspect of yourself. You must personally discover the meaning of life. Once you find your life's meaning, you will use it as a focal point for your existence and as a standard to assess future life choices.

To Fathers

We can't take anyone into the manhood journey further than we have gone ourselves, so you are expected to read ahead, prepare for the discussion, and be able to describe your beliefs and feelings in an honest and vulnerable way. It is important that you lead this most significant process well. This means that you are able to choose to do what is needed in order to heal the wounds that are a result of all that you did not receive from the adult males in your life. Knights of the 21st Century is a knighthood course for men. It has been used successfully in churches, schools, civic clubs, and prisons to help men, who have never been through a manhood process, gain insight into what a man is, how God made him, and what it means to be a man in the 21st century. As a supplement to this book, consider finding a group of men in your church or community with whom you can go on your own manhood walk. Knights of the 21st Century can help you with this quest. As you experience your own manhood experience, you will be even better prepared to help your son on his manhood journey.

Judges 13:8 states, "Then [a man named] Manoah prayed to the LORD. He said, 'Lord, I beg you to let the man of God you sent to us come again. He told us we would have a son. We want the man of God to teach us how to bring up the boy.'" You have been gifted with a son or a young male to mentor. There are few things in this world that are more important than doing a good job in this area. The future of your family, your legacy, and the world hinges on your dedication to this task. Go for it! Work on your own manhood journey and give a young male in your life the gift of manhood, which will help him long after your presence in his life has ended. We have developed a website that will be helpful in supporting both of you. Please register your intent to take your son into this program by emailing us at bull@knightsofthe21stcentury.com. We would like to help you succeed in this journey.

In the assignments at the end of each chapter, you will be asked to create an experience with your son in which you take ownership of the nature of your relationship so far. This frank conversation will create a "give and take" honesty that will set the stage for your son's manhood journey and prepare you both to take your relationship to deeper levels, should you choose to add *Being God's Man* to your son's life. It may also be helpful for you to review the content of the survey found at the end of this book. You can prepare yourself for what is expected as you model, for your son, the importance of honest self-evaluation, the acceptance of imperfection as a necessary part of a growth process and the value that other men add to your life through their support.

At the end of *Being God's Man*, we will discuss a graduation program that will serve as the ceremony that initiates your son into manhood. Most of us have never had a ceremony that took us from childhood to manhood. There is a desire in all of us to achieve a level of responsibility that includes an expectation for adult behaviors and responses from a specific point on. *Bull* and *Being God's Man* create an opportunity for this to occur. Your involvement in this opportunity makes all the difference. The *Bull* team can set up a process for your male son to become a man, but your leadership will make this process happen. Tell him what you think, share your successes and failures with him, give him permission to be different from you, focus this time together on him, stick with him during his process of change, and may God bless your journey together.

To All Readers

This book is aimed at communicating with those who are of the younger generation, sometimes known as "generation Y" or "echo boomers." As such, the authors have purposely written in a manner that is closer to the spoken language of this younger generation, using colloquialisms and idiomatic speech patterns that are common. We believe that most young men may not want to read another book written in "textbook speak." We have used the New International Reader's Version of the *Bible* when quoting verses. If you have questions regarding our beliefs, assumptions and motivations, please feel free to study our website at knights21.com or contact us by email at bull@knightsofthe21stcentury.com.

Introduction

If the title of this book did its job, then you did what your parents taught you never to do, and judged a book by its cover. Let's face it, guys will always be guys; no matter how old they get, how mature they become, or how much wisdom and knowledge they have. There will always be a small part of us that likes things that are a bit, well, crude. So, being a guy, as you were sifting through all the books on all the shelves at the bookstore, looking for something that didn't have a title like *A Girl's Dream* or *One Romantic Night*, you stumbled across a book that had the potential to have a few concepts in it that were geared more towards manliness and things guys enjoy, rather than your typical romance novel or overly girly, made-up story where it ends with the words "happily ever after."

I am sad to inform you that this book is not meant to have another four letter word after it, but instead is short for *Bull Elephant*. That's right; this book was inspired by an elephant – go figure. For those of you who are still with me after realizing that this book's title is not what 99.99% of you thought it meant, we can discuss how and why this book got its title. One of the biggest mammals in the animal kingdom is the elephant. Elephants, believe it or not, are "pack" animals that tend to stay in groups or herds in order to help protect the weak and thrive as a unit. These massive creatures are very dependent on the group as a whole in order to survive. If the herd is not in sync, it breaks down, and elephants in the herd begin to die off. In most, if not all herds, there is a male elephant that is bigger, faster, and stronger than all of the other elephants. Over time, he has fought many other male elephants to prove his dominance and he has the scars to prove it. He mates with the females of the herd and is the father of the calves of the group. He is considered the top dog, the alpha male, the King Leonidas of his elephant community. He is the BULL Elephant.

For those of you who are *still* with me and have decided that you will give this book a chance at least into Chapter 1, I will continue on with my explanation for the title. I am not telling you to lift a bunch of weights, become massive, find a group of people, and beat up all of the men and keep all the women for yourself *(as appealing as that might sound)*. The bull elephant is more than a massive and intimidating force that scares all of the other elephants into submission and rules over them until he dies. You see, the bull elephant is as wise as he is massive, as smart as he is tough, and as loving as he is courageous. The bull elephant is what we young men should aspire to be: a leader. The bull elephant not only protects the herd from predators, but he teaches the younger males how to do the same. It is the bull elephant that is responsible for the survival of the herd through the next generation. If he fails to do his part and teach the younglings how to keep the herd as a cohesive unit, it will break down and will gradually die off during the younglings' time in power. However, if the bull teaches the young elephants the tools of his trade – responsibility, unity, courage, strength, honesty, and all of his other valuable attributes and personality traits, the herd will survive another generation and continue on its journey in the animal kingdom.

This book was inspired by the true events that took place in the late 1990s, as reported by the BBC News in February 2000, in a game park in eastern South Africa. Game park animals are taken from the wild and placed with other animals in protected game parks in hopes of attracting tourists and saving them from being poached. In this particular park, despite the efforts of the staff to keep all of the animals safe, they began noticing that the rhinos that were placed in the park were dying. Those in charge quickly started tracking down the cause of the rhino deaths. It turned out that it wasn't poachers, disease, or the inability of the rhinos to adapt to their home. Elephants were hunting them down and killing them.

The reason for these unusual deaths was not because elephants are natural born hunters of rhinoceroses, but for an entirely different reason. When taking animals from the wild and placing them in the preservation, the staff brought in 15-year-old elephants, which are considered to be adolescents in elephant years. Those in charge of the park decided that they would bring in six adult bull elephants to be the elders in the herd in hopes of stopping what these younger elephants were doing. It is not quite clear how this was communicated between the older elephants and their younger counterparts, but once the older males were brought in, the killing of rhinoceroses stopped. Somehow, these bull elephants were able to communicate to the young male elephants that random violence towards other animals in the animal kingdom is not a necessary requirement for being a strong male. This is why listening to the Bulls in our life is so important; for if we fail to develop relationships with these types of role models, our youthful energy is likely to become misguided.

Very few males in our society are interested in becoming Bull Elephants. They are very relaxed within their herd, and feel that the role of the Bull is not really that important, or it is beyond their capabilities. They are focused more on the here and now and are not worried about the future. They look out for themselves and think that others should do the same: an every-man-for-himself mentality. They don't listen to others, don't think before speaking, and believe that they are never wrong. They talk a big talk, but when the herd is in danger they never "walk the walk." They are not afraid of hurting other members of the herd in order for their needs to be taken care of first. They think they are special and more important than others.

However, there are a growing number of men who are ready to become Bull Elephants. These men understand the importance of taking care of others and teaching young males the importance of leadership, courage, honesty, and integrity. They are willing to stand firm and do battle against the evil forces crashing in around them. They know that God has prepared them to protect their herd. These men are not afraid to die if it means serving a greater cause. They admit when they are wrong, and they take risks because they understand that these types of situations give them a chance to learn and grow. They understand that by venturing off into the unknown, they are helping their herd press on toward a greater future. They do not like sitting still. They believe a man should never be 100% comfortable, because if he is, it means that he is not doing everything that he could. They are always willing to put their lives on the line (both figuratively and literally) for the good of the herd, and expect nothing in return for their deeds. These men are the true Bull Elephants.

What happens in a world where there are no Bulls? We only have to look at inner-city gangs to see what happens when there are no men who serve as positive role models. Left to their own devices, young males move in the direction of violence, as it is considered manly. Manhood is then diminished to the lowest common denominator because the young males do not understand how to set standards for themselves without positive role models. Self-improvement is put aside, because long-term thinking appears to be irrelevant. What feels good at this moment, no matter how harmful it could be to himself and others, is what takes precedence over doing the right thing in the face of wrongdoing.

As Bull Elephants guide their young, so did Paul guide the youthful Timothy. 1 Timothy 4:12 states, "Don't let anyone look down on you because you are young. Set an example for the believers in what you say and in how you live. Also set an example in how you love and in what you believe. Show the believers how to be pure." In order to become a youthful leader such as this, you need to find Bull Elephants who you can respect. In 1 Timothy 3, it states, "If anyone wants to be a leader in the church, he wants to do a good work for God and people." As a young man, you should seek to become the leader that God has called you to be. The end of this story is that someday, you will grow tusks and become a Bull Elephant to others who need your leadership.

When does the journey to becoming a Bull Elephant begin? The answer is "now." Applying what you learn from this book regarding life's truths helps you start this journey. What is true in the animal kingdom holds true in our lives as men: It is only a matter of time before those who observe you begin to exclaim that you are a man who deserves respect. By following in the footsteps of the Bulls before us, one day, we too will become powerful leaders of men.

Manhood Discussion Instructions

To make steel strong, you must heat it. These questions can serve as fuel, creating the heat that is necessary to help each of you become as strong and resilient as possible. As you answer the questions at the end of each chapter, please follow these instructions:

1. The son gets 1st dibs on which of you answers each question first.

2. Each person must recognize that honesty is expected, but how much you share with each other is your choice.

3. It is more important to have a quality man-to-man discussion than to answer each question in its entirety.

4. Each person's thought process and opinion is to be respected. It is expected that there will be times when you will "agree to disagree."

5. As a manhood team, you can choose to deal with these questions in any order. You can decide together whether to skip any of them. It is important to push each other's growth process as much as possible.

Introduction

1. Identify three ways that you see women and men as being similar and three ways you see them as different.

2. As you observe life, identify four ways that teenage males get into trouble. If you could each talk to all of the young teenage males in the world and give them two messages, what would those messages be?

3. When you look at your family or others (your herd) that you spend time with, what are the issues that you need to consider, as the Bull Elephant or future Bull Elephant of your herd regarding your responsibility to protect them?

4. Identify three characteristics that a leader of people should have. Grade yourself on the attributes that are on each other's lists. If you want to be courageous, grade yourself on the attributes on your own list.

5. 1 Timothy 4:12 states, "Don't let anyone look down on you because you are young. Set an example for the believers in what you say and in how you live. Also set an example in how you love and in what you believe. Show the believers how to be pure." Apply this *Bible* verse to your discussion of this chapter.

Huc Venite Pueri Ut Viri Sitis: "Here Enter Boys To Become Men"

Being a young man, I grew up with a bit of a chip on my shoulder. If I was a betting man, I'd say chances are you did as well. Let's face it, young men have it really hard in our society, and what's worse is that few people ever recognize our daily struggles. Everyone is always focused on other things like bullying in schools, helping kids reach their goal of a higher education, animal rights campaigns, anti-deforestation committees, and so on. Our nation has come to the conclusion that "boys will be boys" and that what you see is what you get. We are seen as nothing more than walking drones, with the emotional capacity of a paper bag, who run around outside, get muddy, play sports, spit, and fish.

As it turns out, young men have it pretty hard. We are hard-wired to be extremely curious, and from our first second on this planet, we are exploring, whether our exploration is for hidden treasure, a friend, a wife, truth, or knowledge. Sadly, a lot of young men are not surrounded by Bull Elephants who teach them core values, honesty, integrity, and truth. We are forced to venture off on our own and figure this world out for ourselves. When we are taught something, it is the skewed vision of our weakened society and not the caveman instinct that is inside each of us. In school, we are scolded for not being able to sit still; in church, we are forced to hold hands and sing songs about a strange man who hangs out with sheep and are rarely taught the manly side of Jesus. You know Jesus, the guy who fought back against those who were corrupting the church, the man who spent 30 days alone in the desert, and the man who was

1

willing to die for each and every one of us. Our parents quickly lash out at us when we come home muddy, and we are punished for being "too aggressive" in sports. Young boys are given opposite messages: They are not told how they can express their feelings or beliefs in a manly way, so they use their fists instead. At the same time they are reprimanded for being too physical and they are also told that they need to express their emotions through communication rather than physical confrontation. Many of our male role models remain silent, so it is no wonder why these young boys have no clue how to act.

Testicular fortitude is an attribute that many adults forget to teach young men when forging them into adults. Boys and young men need to be taught to stand up for themselves, protect those they love, and remain steadfast in the face of evil. This courage, this drive to do the right thing and not be scared of what others will say, is simply left out of the equation. As young boys are pushed down the assembly line of life, the authority figures decide that it is too time-consuming and costly to add in courage while helping them build character. When we come off the assembly line, we look like we should and are worthy of our place in the display case as handsome young men. But something under the hood is missing and in a few year's time, people really start to notice that these machines are running poorly.

I am not saying that we learn nothing in school or from our teachers and coaches; however, there are no classes that teach boys how to become men. So, instead, we turn toward boys who are older than us, watch them, and ask them for advice. Sadly, we have no idea that our authority figures skipped courage when developing them as well. These guys have no clue that their authority figures are too scared to discipline them. They treat the young males around them in simplistic ways. These boys are treated like delicate flowers and are never disciplined; their exception is that it might damage them. They are dumbed down and not expected to know what their God-given design is, let alone develop it. This lack of discipline leads young boys to a life with little to no self-control, self-respect, or ability to accomplish the goals that could stretch them toward becoming men. Luckily, there are a growing number of men who are going back to their caveman roots, preaching the Word of God, and teaching these impressionable young boys what it truly means to become a man, and more importantly, a man of God. There is no mathematical equation, scientific method or specific formula for creating the ultimate man of God, and this leads many people to choose to avoid the daunting challenge of mentoring young boys. To father or mentor properly, those who are older must become personally involved. Our male society has become scared of the difficult task of helping young males become men. They cannot possibly teach these young boys courage, integrity, honesty, love, passion, and what it takes to be a man. They would rather hide behind excuses such as "it takes too much time," or "maybe later," or "someone else will take care of it." Sadly, along with useless excuses that do not cut it, the males in our society blame these young boys for their inadequacy as leaders. Some authority figures try to sell the idea that there is something screwed up with today's youth, and it is just too difficult to teach them any differently. These fathers and mentors cover up for their lack of manhood by shifting the responsibility for these young males, placing it solely on their sons. They hide behind excuses when reality is much different. It's time for more men to step up to the plate and start to prepare these young boys for battle, to sculpt them into hardened warriors, and to turn them into men of God. Fathers and mentors who become part of this manhood journey will prove that a new way is possible.

During my senior year of high school, I decided to try out for the school track team. The head coach and distance coach was a man by the name of Charles Harrison, or Coach, as I call him. A United States Marine with an intimidating disposition and extremely high standards, Coach was the ultimate role model. Coach Harrison was the first Bull in my life outside of my family. You see, this man was such a strong example of a leader to me, that now, several years after running for him, I still refer to him as Coach. The amount of respect this man earned from me is shown in my inability to call him by his first name or even Mr. Harrison. He doesn't ask me to call him Coach, but it is hard-wired in me. This Bull Elephant is seen so highly in my eyes that I can't shake the true image of him – a true leader, my coach. So, to all of you males out there who have a slight heartache, wishing that someone, somewhere, would look up to you; it's as simple as being a Bull Elephant.

As a competitor, I wanted to run for Coach Harrison, knowing that he would push me towards accomplishments that I could define as great. Very quickly, I found myself as one of the legs for our 4x800 (referred to as 4x8 in track and field) meter relay team. Coach required us to start our training in November, for a season that only began the following March. As we approached the tail end of our season, our relay team was on the verge of making it to the Pennsylvania State Track & Field Meet, a pinnacle event in track and field. This is an annual invitational meet for only the top runners, throwers, and jumpers in Pennsylvania; it is an event that very few kids from my high school were ever invited to attend. Coach did everything by the numbers (from carbohydrate intake to the amount of water we should be drinking every day to the exact mileage and time that we needed to run each day) and made sure our 4x8 relay team was right on track *(no pun intended)* with where we needed to be. As we approached the races to qualify for the state meet, we had to pick up our training a bit, which meant long runs on Saturdays (up to 10 miles). It was my last long Saturday run before our team's final season meet and the final determining factor on which our selection for the state meet hinged.

Five miles out, five miles back. *Easy enough, right?* As I started out on my run, I noticed that the sky was growing rather dark, the wind was picking up just a bit, and I swear I heard the voice of Mother Nature saying "Just turn back, kid." However, I told myself I'd beat the storm, be back before the heavy rain came, and that Mother Nature was just a big talker and didn't really mean what she said. I was in the flow of my run, very relaxed and feeling at peace. That is, until I hit mile 5 and turned around. At that very moment, Mother Nature decided that any young buck who wasn't intimidated by her soft words of warning needed to be forced into submission with her iron fist, which came in the form of rain, wind, hail, thunder, and lightning.

After running for Coach for a number of months, I was starting to be as hard-nosed as he was and I was not going to let Mother Nature prevent me from completing my training for the day. I told her to kiss my back side and continued running back toward home. When I reached mile 7 or 8, I quickly learned that Mother Nature is easily offended and she will make you pay for insulting her. The wind, rain, and hail continued to pick up, quite dramatically, to the point where I could not see more than a foot in front of me. Finally, after what seemed like hours, bogged down by my soaking wet clothes, waterlogged shoes, and a rather "annoyed" attitude in respect to Mother Nature, I saw a truck, and just assumed that the driver would pick me up because of how awful the storm was. Well, apparently Mother Nature called the driver of this truck, told him how terrible of a person I was, and advised him to stay away from me or she'd come after him as well. Needless to say, the driver of the truck didn't stop, or even slow down; he just drove right on by.

That next Monday as I walked into Coach's office, he asked me how my run in the hail storm was. Still a bit upset about my luck, I quickly fired back, asking him how he knew when I was on my run. He, calmly and with a sheepish grin on his face, explained to me, that he was the person in the truck who drove by me without showing any intention of slowing down or picking me up. How on earth could this man drive by me in that kind of weather and not pick me up?! His answer was simple, "There is no such thing as bad weather, just weak people." After a few choice words that I won't repeat to you, I stormed out of his room thinking he was nothing more than a lunatic who was probably suffering from Post Traumatic Stress Disorder (PTSD) and needed prompt psychological help. But Coach wasn't insane; he was a Bull Elephant.

He made me run in the worst conditions to make certain I was prepared to be even that much better when I was running in excellent conditions. You see, Coach knew that this ten-mile run had very little impact on my physical strength when it was added to the hundreds of miles that I had already run during that season. What he wanted me to develop was mental toughness. He understood that, in my epic battle against Mother Nature, I could have cut my run short, been driven home, and I would have missed out on a mile or two of training *or* I could stick it out, suck it up, and develop the mental toughness that was needed for the final, most challenging days of my season. Our 4x8 relay team made it to the state meet and set the school record in the process, all thanks to my Coach, this Bull, and what he taught us.

I told you this story to encourage you to face life like Coach made me face the weather. Do not let life, and those in it, intimidate you. With willpower, determination, courage, and trust in God, you can face any of life's hail storms, run through them, and go on to accomplish great things. A man learns to suck up the pain in order to reach his goals. James 1: 2-5 states,

> My brothers and sisters, you will face all kinds of trouble. When you do, think of it as pure joy. Your faith will be put to the test. You know that when that happens it will produce in you the strength to continue. The strength to keep going must be allowed to finish its work. Then you will be all you should be. You will have everything you need. If any of you need wisdom, ask God for it. He will give it to you. God gives freely to everyone. He doesn't find fault.

I encourage you to face life's trials and hardships like I eventually embraced the storm. Have faith in God and understand that when He tests your faith, you are gaining stamina. When you make it through any hardship in life, you are building endurance to run through the next obstacle that life throws your way. I trained for months under Coach for a race that took me less than two minutes. Why? Because men understand that the triumph greatly outweighs the pain and suffering that you endure in order to prepare for the race. You will also find this to be true for your manhood journey; all the pain and suffering that you experience along the way will be well worth it once you achieve manhood.

Manhood Discussion - Chapter 1

1. What are you angry about that is occurring around you? Is there something that you do that makes life more difficult?

2. Identify five core values that a man should consider when making a decision. Identify a person who lives according to each principle. Identify a person who violates each of these principles.

3. How would each of you define the phrase "men of God?" Is this a goal that you have for yourself?

4. Identify a storm in life during which you had to "gut it out" in order to get through it in a manly manner. Share a possible storm or two that you both may face in the future. Who can you rely on to help you through these challenging times?

5. James 1:2-5 states,

> My brothers and sisters, you will face all kinds of trouble. When you do, think of it as pure joy. Your faith will be put to the test. You know that when that happens it will produce in you the strength to continue. The strength to keep going must be allowed to finish its work. Then you will be all you should be. You will have everything you need. If any of you need wisdom, ask God for it. He will give it to you. God gives freely to everyone. He doesn't find fault.

Apply these *Bible* verses to your discussion of this chapter. How is the building up of wisdom connected to the trials you experience in life?

A Lesson From The Wisdom Muffin: Use Your Left Foot

2

Wisdom Muffin? Yes, Wisdom Muffin. That's a nick-name that's been given to my father by his friends and family. For example, in a group which is having a furious discussion, he will speak very little; but when he does it's an utterance of, well, WISDOM! There's no denying it. He is the wisest human being that I know. Throughout this book I'll refer to him as Father, Dad, Pop, and the Wisdom Muffin. One day I hope to earn the same respected title from my friends, colleagues, and family.

One of my first gifts, as a child, was a soccer ball. One of my first memories was getting a pair of soccer cleats. And my childhood is riddled with memories of weekend soccer tournaments, exciting games, dramatic upsets and last minute triumphs. Being an active youngster, I was always bugging my dad to come play in the backyard with me, hoping to school him in the game I loved and show him how much I was improving. He would oblige and let me whoop his backside for a while, until he grew tired. "Alright," he'd say, "Now practice with your left foot." HA! This so-called Wisdom Muffin wanted me to practice with my left foot? No one ever practiced with their weaker foot. It was a waste of time and took away from the time I needed for practicing with my dominant foot. Not to mention, it was boring and difficult.

A decade and a half later, during a summer league before my senior year, I found myself being carried off the pitch *(field, for you non-soccer players)* with my right ankle the size of a grapefruit, thinking my season was over. I went up for a header against my opponent and we crashed into each other. I came crashing down on my ankle, felt an instantaneous shooting pain, and heard several popping sounds. I was certain that the sound, tremendous pain, and look of discomfort on my opponent's face was an indication that my ankle was broken and my senior season was over before it had started. My entire life had been spent practicing, training, running, lifting, and then practicing some more, all for the love of this game, only to find myself ready to "ride some pine" during my final season.

Amazingly, after only a few short weeks, I was able to play again, thanks to the efforts of our school's personal trainer, an athletic director who helped me through an excellent rehabilitation program. However, my ankle was not the same. I needed to wear an ankle brace for every game, and wrap it in about half a roll of athletic tape. I spent my nights lying on the couch icing my swollen ankle and taking pain medication like it was candy. I was in tremendous pain for most of the day, limped around school, and tried to convince my coaches and athletic trainers of how good I felt, so I would not be forced to sit out the game. Needless to say, my once strong, accurate, and dominant foot which I had relied on for my entire life, was now fragile and painful; it was serving only as a support to keep my body upright on the field.

As it turns out, my father was right *(as usual)*; even though I hated all of those hours in the backyard practicing ball control with my left foot, it paid off. Instead of losing my spot on the starting line-up, due to be-ing limited to my non-dominant foot, I was able to keep my spot as our starting forward. Thanks to my father's words of wisdom, I had begun practicing ball control and flexibility with my left foot at an early age. Because of this training, I was able to be just as effective a player as I was before my injury. I helped my team that year, but if it wasn't for my dad and his constant badgering to practice with my left foot, I would have been a much weaker player after I injured my right foot. In fact, I am certain that I would have lost my starting spot and spent most of the season watching the game from the sidelines. I would have been a joke to my opponents, and my coach would have seen me as a hindrance to our team's success. But, due to all of that hard work and the encouragement I received from my pop, I was a threat to my opponents and was able to support my teammates and coach, even with a bum ankle.

I know my father and I know that every lesson he teaches me has two purposes. First, he really wanted me to learn to use my weaker foot. Not only does it make you a better athlete when you are ambidextrous, but practicing with your non-dominant foot (or hand) actually improves the coordination of your dominant one. *Wild, right?* More importantly, like all of my father's words of advice, he had something else in mind. When he encouraged me to practice with my left foot, he wasn't just showing me how to become a better soccer player. He was also showing me the importance of working beyond my self-defined comfort zone. A person does not grow or develop new skills when the work that is being done stays within their comfort level. But, if pushed or forced to go just a *little bit* outside of that comfort zone, talent begins to show and skills begin to develop.

So gentlemen, I am extending my father's words of wisdom to you by encouraging you to use your left foot, whether it is in the game of soccer or the game of life. Push yourself, even if it's just a little bit. Practice with your non-dominant foot or anything else that you are uncomfortable with, or that you would like to succeed in, and watch your "dominant foot" grow even stronger. You will never soar to great heights if your primary goal in life is to be comfortable. It is only when you are pushing yourself mentally, physically, or spiritually past your limits that you will notice your successes start to stack up.

Most males are willing to work on things they are already good at. It may even be in an area that they do not mind spending hours practicing or training; or for a skillset they once mastered during their younger years. In order for a man to show what he is really made of, he needs to choose to develop the areas of life in which he is less skilled and not avoid them. Does he have the self-control and self-discipline to push himself past his limits? Men do not like to lose or to appear weak because we all have a part of ourselves called an ego (our pride). When we decide to practice a certain skill to strengthen it (whether that skill is practicing with our left foot or working on our lack of patience), we may believe that we are showing our Achilles' heel to those around us. If we let our ego/pride control us, how can we become good at anything? I wasn't immediately skilled with my left foot; it took me hundreds of hours, all the while being willing to try, and often fail, before I was able to excel on the pitch. It takes a man to decide, "Am I willing to fail repeatedly in order to get better?" I wanted to become better at soccer, so I was willing to screw up thousands of times, look like an idiot, and practice the same moves over and over again, in order to make certain that when game time came, I would nail the move perfectly and help my team win the game. Start practicing in the areas of your life that need improvement. Instead of fearing failure, learn to make it your friend. Failure doesn't define you; what you do with failure is what defines you. Suck up your pride and don't be afraid of looking like an idiot, especially if it means that you are working on areas that will make you into a stronger man. Keep working hard; stay committed; eventually the countless hours of working on your weaknesses will pay off.

One of the keys to the growth of the relationship between a father and a son (or mentor and mentee) is spending time together. This time should be spent on activities where there is mutual respect because lessons will not be learned if the son feels dominated. He needs to feel his dad's guidance. My dad created a compromise between what I *wanted* and what I *needed*. Because of this, I was able to enjoy the memories I have of beating him in one-on-one soccer matches. Those lessons prepared me to accept the importance of using my weaker foot; it also provided me with a lesson that I would use at a later point in my life: to work at developing myself in areas that are uncomfortable to me.

In John 10:10, Jesus promises, "I have come so they can have life. I want them to have it in the fullest possible way." To achieve this, as men, we must do some things in life that are quite uncomfortable, but through our suffering will come great triumph. We must take ownership of our weaker attributes and devote ourselves to a greater being for this triumph to be reached. Fathers, coaches, and God are there to help us, push us, and watch us as we grow toward manhood. We must submit our will to God which is an important part of our growth process and learn to use the gifts that are as poorly developed as my left foot. We never know when an accident or a life challenge will come our way; what we do know is that having a good relationship with our father and mentors can help support us through these hardships in life.

In the *Bible* it says, "Everyone has sinned. No one measures up to God's glory" (Romans 3:23). We are all imperfect and have "left feet" that need improvement. The relationship Christ is offering each one of us can help us push through our comfort zones, as boys, and become the men of God who He has called us to be. It is my goal to encourage you to start establishing your manhood and your faith in Jesus, and work to improve your relationship with your father. We must wave goodbye to the parts of our lives where we feel comfortable, and venture into the unknown with our father by our side. You are both tough enough to test your relationship and by doing this, take it deeper. Answering the questions at the end of each chapter together will help you do this. The decision to leave your comfort zone behind will require you to begin having a more open relationship with each other. It also will mean exploring possibly painful or uncomfortable zones with each other by discussing issues in your life that you may have avoided up until now.

Manhood Discussion - Chapter 2

1. When you look at your life, identify two life skills that you think you are good at and which come easily to you.

2. Identify a life skill that you want to develop. What can you do to practice (with your left foot) this life skill so that you can achieve it?

3. Identify a failure that you have experienced. How did you react to this failure?

4. Discuss with each other how you would like to handle the failures you experience in the future.

5. Romans 3:23 states, "Everyone has sinned. No one measures up to God's glory." What does this *Bible* verse mean in relation to the topic of this chapter?

One Warning, Two Cats

Before I go any further in this book and start sharing the really important stuff, I am going to issue a warning to each of you who are reading it. The results that you see exploring the concepts in this book are not immediate; they are not externally visible, and come with no certificate of accomplishment. You cannot physically show your neighbor, coworker, or friends at school what you will gain from this book *(However, they will see your actions become more man-like)*. The changes are all internal and you will become increasingly aware that you are a work in progress. Turning the last page in this book is not the end of your training. I don't want to sound corny by reusing an old cliché, but I am going to say it anyway: When you finish reading this book, it is not the end, but the beginning. If you can sift through my words, paragraph after paragraph, page after page, pick up a thing or two, and finally complete this book, you are then ready to start your adventure into manhood. Your dad can help you take the first step through the door to manhood, but ultimately it is up to you to take your manhood to the next level.

I have two cats, Donald Meichenbaum and Harry Stack Sullivan *(The names are a product of growing up with a psychologist for a father)*. At least once a day, one of my cats decides that his tail is an evil sorcerer, and he is the only hope left to save all of humanity. He accepts the difficult task of protecting the human race and embarks on an epic battle with his tail to the death! He spins around rapidly, trying desperately to capture his foe, The Tail, and lets it be known that it will not rule the earth. Once he finally catches his evil tail, he begins chomping on it with vigor and a great deal of triumph in his eye. That is, until suddenly, out of nowhere, a rolled up paper ball gives him a dirty look and needs to be thwarted as well! My cat lunges at this new and even more dangerous foe, and begins to let the paper ball tough guy know who is boss.

Now, some of you might have just asked yourselves, "Why on earth am I reading an entire paragraph about cats doing cat things?" There is an underlying point behind this story of two creatures with the combined IQ of 17. My cats have the attention span of a few seconds. They understand what is going on right this second, but nothing past that. They have no concept of tomorrow, next week, next year, or even the next few minutes.

I want to advise you not to be like a cat. We live in a society where everything is immediate, including fast food, internet, texting, Skype, and everything in between. All of it is brought to you in half a second or less. You can find almost any kind of information on the internet at blazing fast speeds, information that took your father and grandfather days, or even weeks of searching books at the library *(whatever a library is)*. We expect immediate gratification and cannot stand being told to wait around. We want it, and we want it *now*. We hate doing things in ways that delay our gratification. If we cannot see immediate results, we figure it is a waste of time or that we are doing something wrong and should just give up.

Cats make excellent house pets, but they make terrible leaders. Don't be like a cat. Please understand that the most important things in life take time and must be constantly worked on and monitored. This adventure WILL take time and if you do not see results within the next five minutes, you must press on. I promise you that tomorrow will come and you will grow slowly, day by day, until you are a powerful leader of men!

For those of you who need a more serious explanation than a cat waging war against its tail, I will give you a brief, but more serious example. Take a clear glass and fill it to the top with water. Each day, take some red dye and put only one drop into the glass of water. Notice that, at first, the water color doesn't change much, if at all. In fact, at one drop a day, it could take you a few days to a few weeks to start noticing a difference. However, if you keep at it, day after day, eventually the clear glass of water will turn bright red. Similarly, you need to understand that gaining wisdom, searching for truth, and seeking knowledge is not going to happen immediately. Like the red dye in the glass of water, becoming a man, and more importantly a Christian man, takes time. Even if you don't notice it right away, each day of practice and training will pay off until your true colors of wisdom, knowledge, truth, and honesty are displayed proudly for everyone to see.

Men and males everywhere are constantly willing to push themselves to the edge when it comes to external man-like activities such as hiking, fishing, sports, cars, tools, and the like. However, when it comes to inward-focused man-like topics, males, and even a few men, are much more hesitant to push themselves past their comfort levels. No man, male, or boy wants to be beaten at anything that is considered manly by others. For this reason, men are always competing in sports and other physical activities. Ever watch three guys stand around a grill? There is often some kind of verbal competition centering around how to make the best burgers, and usually each man has a secret technique that is better than the other's. Isn't it interesting how we will more easily attach our passion to our external skills, the skills that others can see and measure, rather than our internal strength? The problem is, when it comes to internal manliness, guys everywhere never try to compete. You will never hear a male bragging about the work he is doing on his own internal weaknesses, such as being a better father. You also won't hear a male talk about apologizing to other males when he is wrong. Males don't do that. Men do. It is time that we, as men, turn our passion toward what matters most, our "insides"; as we build our character, it is better to develop our knowledge, capabilities and skills within ourselves.

Shane, a guy I respect more than most, is one of the younger Bulls in my life. He might not have the same life experience as the older, more mature Bulls. However, the things he does know, he knows well. Shane is always willing to share his advice with me and does so in an easy to understand fashion. Shane grew up as a wrestler and a football star and began to learn his way around the gym at a young age. When I first met Shane, he taught me the ropes of working out and how to alter my lifting program depending on my desired goals. Being a skinny kid growing up, I wanted to stack on some weight in hope of not looking like I was 12 years old for the rest of my life.

Shane helped me every step of the way and not only helped me get a bit bigger, but more importantly he helped me get a lot stronger as well. The greatest piece of advice Shane ever gave me when it came to working out was quite simple; in fact, it was only one word: *squat*. So, gentlemen, I too, am going to encourage you to squat. When it comes to weight-lifting, most guys like lifting the "show me" muscles; the curls for the girls and the chest for the chicks motto has been in the gym for years. When guys work out, they want to lift the muscles that everyone will see in hopes of showing off the progress they are making. However, if you look at the guys with barrel size chests and massive, bulging biceps, I am almost certain *(unless they are smart and lift to become stronger, not just to show off)* that their legs look like chicken legs. These guys spend so much time focusing on their bench press and bicep curl that they neglect to take time out to lift one of, if not the most important muscle groups, the legs.

The science side of squatting is actually pretty straightforward. Much of a man's testosterone is stored in his quads. However, Shane gave an explanation about the importance of squatting a bit differently which makes perfect sense. Shane explained, "Look at any house, then look at its frame, or its foundation. Is it weak and skinny? No. If you want a strong, sturdy house, you must build a strong and sturdy foundation. Like a house, a man must build his foundation, or his legs, in order to support his upper body." Once I started squatting and taking it seriously, my overall strength shot up, as well as my muscle mass and my overall body weight.

Becoming a man is like squatting. Its extraordinarily painful, requires a lot of practice and dedication, and no one really notices the muscle development from a squat. But, if you train hard, keep at it, and push yourself to keep adding weight, you will start to become a man and you will grow mentally and spiritually in the right direction. Don't let the lack of outward signs thwart you from continuing your path to manhood, and understand that whether others can see it or not, if you continue to train and stay focused, you will become a true man.

Matthew 7:24-27 states,

> So then everyone who hears my words and puts them into practice is like a wise man. He builds his house on the rock. The rain comes down. The water rises. The winds

16

blow and beat against that house. But it does not fall. It is built on the rock. But everyone who hears my words and does not put them into practice is like a foolish man. He builds his house on the sand. The rain comes down. The water rises. The winds blow and beat against that house. And it falls with a loud crash.

This passage shows that when it comes to important life issues, great importance must be placed on developing a solid foundation on which to build. In order to build a Christian man, there is an activity, like the squat, that is often overlooked. It is reading the *Bible*. In 1 Timothy 4:13, Paul tells young Timothy, "Until I come, spend your time reading Scripture out loud to one another. Spend your time preaching and teaching." It seems hard to read the *Bible* consistently, but as young men who want to walk with God, we must read it. This type of discipline, when approached regularly with an open heart, can provide amazing strength that permeates our lives. Although, at times, the *Bible* can seem confusing, you need to do as 1 Corinthians 2:10 reminds us to do. It teaches us that it is the spirit of God that understands all things and that God is there to help us understand the deeper things of the scriptures, if we simply wait on Him. In the *Bible*, there are many examples of men who have failed, and of the ways that God used their willingness to change to accomplish great things. As you read the *Bible*, try to listen to God because He will talk to you during this time. His Spirit will connect with your spirit as you meditate on a proverb, read an Old Testament story, or think about the words of Christ. Trying to be a man without the Christian squat will limit your ability to be your best.

Manhood Discussion - Chapter 3

1. Identify the ways that you want to be different as a result of this manhood process. What are three characteristics of a man? Do you have the patience, as with the red dye example, to create this change in your life?

2. How hard is it for you to delay gratification and say "No" to an impulse? Identify four things that are hard for you to wait for. How has the choice not to delay your gratification affected you in the past?

3. Discuss what you think about pushing the edge and growing on the outside. What does it mean to push the edge and grow on the inside?

4. Identify one area/attribute that you could work on in order to become more of a man. What kind of plan could you develop which would help you with this growth area?

5. 1 Timothy 4:13 states, "Until I come, spend your time reading Scripture out loud to one another. Spend your time preaching and teaching." How does this *Bible* verse relate to the topic of this chapter?

Go West, Young Man

When I decided I wanted to write a book asking young gents to turn themselves into hardened men, I knew I would have to ask myself to do the same. I promised myself this would not be a "Do as I say, not as I do" kind of thing, and that whatever I asked my readers to do, I would have already done, or would be currently attempting myself. The great men in my life, who I have dubbed Bull Elephants, have never asked me to do something that they themselves have not done, and I hold these men in great regard. Rather than dictating and commanding others to do what they could not, they forged the path themselves, allowing others to follow them into the unknown. Manhood, at times, is inconvenient, for it demands that we "practice what we preach." Along with you, I am also attempting to do what these phenomenal leaders did for me and want to preface what is to come in this book with a promise: I promise each and every one of you that at no point during the suggestions that I give in this book will I ask you to do something that I have been too scared to attempt myself.

From his very first breath, every man has a passion that burns within him, which urges him to push himself to his limits and beyond. He is constantly striving to push past his comfort zone and dive head first into a world of uncertainty. He wants to dominate the unknown and prove to himself that he has what it takes to push himself harder and further than anyone else could possibly push him. He understands that through struggle comes strength and through pain comes pride. He holds himself to a higher standard than he holds others, for he knows that by doing so, he can grow physically, mentally, and spiritually.

With that being said, we must gain a common understanding of what our "limits" are, and what it means to push past them. Every man has his limits, or *edge*. Each man constantly strives to push himself toward them. If men were complacent about being comfortable, very little would get accomplished. But because there are brave men who are willing to venture into a world of pain, struggle, and uncertainty, great deeds are accomplished. Whether these men are like the explorers of old, a soldier at war, a father at home, or a friend in need, they are constantly searching for their edge and walking, *(no, running)* toward it. Every man's edge is different, and I knew I would have to find mine.

Growing up as an athlete, I was always very comfortable with sports. I played soccer and basketball, ran track, was always at ease in gym class, and developed a great appreciation for weight-lifting in my late teens and early twenties. At first, I thought I would push myself to the edge by entering a triathlon, the epitome of physical fitness. After searching inside myself carefully, asking God for His guidance, and talking with a few Bull Elephants in my life, I realized that this was not my edge. I was too comfortable with athletics and physical fitness. I would not learn much about my character if I focused on an area that, for me, was safe.

As I continued to search inward in an attempt to figure out what my manhood test would be, God decided to step in and work His wonders. God, more times than not, works in mysterious ways, and looking back on what happened, I now understand that God had decided that He would help me find my edge. One of my closest friends on this planet, and a gentleman I consider to be a brother, Jamie, approached me one day, asking if I wanted to go on a bit of an adventure the summer after our college graduation. Jamie, along with another very close friend, Rook, and one of my roommates, Evan, was planning to take a trip out to Glacier National Park, located in Montanna, to hike in the back country for a few weeks. Hiking and camping is not the frontier for these three men, as they grew up doing this sort of thing all the time. However, for a kid who grew up playing soccer year round and never had time to learn the ropes of camping, I realized that this adventure would certainly take me out of my comfort zone.

That's right! I accepted an invitation to go on a trip to Glacier National Park, in the summer of 2012, to hike for 12 days when I had never once been camping, even in my own backyard! It was a 46-hour car ride, cramped in with three other dudes, followed by almost two weeks of hiking without a home cooked meal, bathroom, or shower, in a place where there were warnings of bear attacks, wolf sightings, and numerous other things that I had never been exposed to, and which are considered to be pretty dang dangerous. This trip had become something I determined I would have to do in order to be truthful with myself when asking others to push themselves towards their edge.

Now, I am not saying that you each need to take a month off from school or work to go backpacking through the woods in order to become a man. I am encouraging you to find an activity that is way beyond your comfort level, whether it is skydiving or running a marathon, reading the *Bible* from front to back or mustering up the courage to ask your boss for a raise. Whatever your biggest limitation is, find it, and go one step further. You will learn that, along with the help of your loved ones and the guidance of Jesus, you can push yourself further than you ever thought possible. My trip was amazing and one that I will never forget. I missed my mom's cooking and my comfortable bed and by the end of the trip, I understood that I will never truly be an outdoorsman. I did, however, teach myself that with God's help and the support of my buddies, I could go further than I once thought. You see, we are often the ones who limit ourselves, and less the obstacles in life.

Many years ago, it was thought that no man could run a mile in under four minutes. Journals and experts proved through scientific measures that it was physically impossible for a man to break a four-minute mile. Then, on a rainy day, when not feeling well, Roger Bannister broke the four-minute barrier. Within the next year, over twenty-five more men succeeded in breaking the barrier as well. The barrier wasn't what was or was not within a young man's ability. The barrier was found in the man's head. I find myself wondering what barriers I have that keep me stuck and have started thinking about how to rise above them. I wonder what barriers you have placed in your mind regarding your future or your ability to walk with God. I believe it is these fears regarding what is impossible for us which have the same validity as was true the day the four-minute mile was broken.

"*HOKA HEY*" is said to have been shouted by Crazy Horse, along with other warriors in his tribe, before battle. "Hoka Hey," which translates into "a great day to die" is a phrase stating that each warrior lived his life in such a way that he had done everything he should have, preceding his last day on earth. Therefore, it was, in fact, a great day to die.

Ever since I heard what "Hoka Hey" meant, I told myself I would hold it close to my heart. To know that you have done all that you could have, or should have, before your last day on this earth, is a core value that men should hold close. My hope is that you, too, can start adopting the mindset of Crazy Horse and approach your final stand with that epic war cry indicating to all of those around you that you have done all you could, and that it is, in fact, a great day to die!

Crazy Horse was and continues to be an iconic symbol to the Native Americans and their fight against the Europeans who started taking over America bit by bit. Crazy Horse was considered by many Native Americans to be a great war hero who would, and did, give his life in the fight against oppression. Now, many years later, the Crazy Horse monument is being erected in his honor. This monument is being carved out of a mountain, yes, a mountain, to honor this brave soldier and tremendous leader. Crazy Horse didn't risk his life in each battle, thinking he would be remembered for generations to come as a leader of men, but because he wanted to protect his people. As potential men, you must understand that you do not need to actively seek glorification from others, but simply be a man. Once you start acting like a real man, your courage, honesty, and integrity will be seen by everyone. You may not get a monument in your honor, but by doing what is right, being a Bull Elephant, and living your life as Crazy Horse did, shouting "HOKA HEY" before every battle, you will be remembered by the loved ones around you, and your teachings will be passed on to your sons. It is not the monument itself that matters, but what that monument represents, that of a man who has lived his life well.

As you read this book, each of you is starting out as a Greenhorn, with fresh legs, excitement about what is to come, and the desire to prove yourself to me, others, and mostly yourself. I, however, do not have a pin, gold star, or medal to give you after you are done with this book. What you will gain from this book (*at least I hope you will*) is internal strength, which no medal or gold star could ever match. External motivation and icons of success fade and deteriorate over time. But that internal strength, that testicular fortitude to press on even when you are at your breaking point, that, my friends, lasts forever.

In the *Bible*, we are reminded of what truly counts in this world. It warns us in Mark 8:36, "What good is it if someone gains the whole world but loses his soul?" "Hoka Hey" was not stated casually by a true warrior, nor did he lay down his life on a whim for something insignificant. There is a way that youth discount their value and because of this, they end up participating in risky behaviors. As a result, many young males die earlier than they should. "Hoka Hey" is an exclamation that lets others know we have value and have lived in a way that doesn't demean us. Psalm 139:14 states, "How you made me is amazing and wonderful. I praise you for that. What you have done is wonderful. I know that very well." "Hoka Hey" states that we are willing to live in ways that show we appreciate the way that God made us to be. It suggests that if our next moment is our last, we have lived our lives, until that moment, according to His will.

Manhood Discussion - Chapter 4

1. Share another experience from your life that took you to your edge. What did you learn from it? Are there any possible choices in your future that would take you to the edge in a good way?

2. Share the names of three good friends that you could rely on if life became difficult.

   Dad: Share a memory of a time when you have been able to rely on your friends. Tell your son the names of the friends you can rely on.

   Son: Identify an activity that would be fun for you and your friends to do together.

3. It has been said, "We are the obstacles to our success." In what ways do you keep yourself from enjoying life and/or accomplishing more? What dynamics or factors are necessary in a situation in order for you to feel like you are in your comfort zone? What "four-minute barrier" limits you in ways that it shouldn't?

4. Discuss what the concept of "Hoka Hey" can mean in your life. What does it take for you to live each day to the fullest? What would you both miss in life if you died today?

5. Mark 8:36 states, "What good is it if someone gains the whole world, but loses his soul?" Apply this *Bible* verse to your discussion of this chapter.

A Lesson From The Wisdom Muffin: Understanding That You Are Terrible With Numbers

5

In second grade, my class had to write a paragraph about what we wanted to be when we grew up. Most of the boys in my class wrote something along the lines of Space Cowboy or Alligator Wrestler. I, on the other hand, went on and on about how I wanted to become a psychologist, just like my father. Ever since I can remember, I wanted to be a shrink just like my old man. My pop was an excellent role model from whom I learned significant amounts of knowledge related to psychology and about life in general. His passion for helping others was firmly instilled in me and I, too, am on a quest to become a psychologist. With my Bachelor's degree complete, I am considering graduate school. For the first eighteen years of my life, I was only subjected to the perks of being a psychologist: You sat in your office which was filled with your books and diplomas, saw your clients, and assisted them in their walk toward recovery. You were the rock in their unstable lives. Thanks to you, people were able to get their lives back on track. What I was not exposed to was the training and schooling that went into becoming a psychotherapist. During the summer after my high school graduation as I was preparing to head off to college, I was extremely excited about the many classes that would teach me what psychology was all about.

One day, toward the end of the summer, my dad and I were driving through town having a great time reminiscing about high school and talking about my excitement about college. My father eventually turned the conversation to a more serious note. He warned me about a side to psychology that I was unaware of, statistics, methods, and applications. Both he and I knew that I was never strong with math or science and that

I struggled with numbers and equations. He told me that a major part of psychology coursework includes gathering statistics and running correlations, and that a lot of psychological-related study deals with research and numbers. He explained to me that there would be a lot of classes I would be required to take where I would find myself studying late at night, ready to internally combust. Boy, was the Wisdom Muffin right! I literally fought my way through these number-filled classes and spent countless hours reading my textbooks, and rereading them and re-rereading them, trying to comprehend information that others saw as a joke. My dad told me this, not to make me feel stupid, or to encourage me to think of a major with less focus on numbers and research, but to encourage me to press on through the hard classes, until I got to the psychology courses which were geared more toward my learning style.

When interviewing for graduate schools and jobs, many people will tell you, "If you are ever asked about your weaknesses, turn them into strengths!" This statement is simply not correct. My father taught me to embrace my weaknesses and use my strengths to combat them. I understand that it will take me twice as long to study for a statistics exam than it does for most other kids. But, I also understand that my determination has been developed to a greater level because of my struggles. I can't turn my weaknesses into strengths, but I can use my strengths to work around my weaknesses. Let's face it, we can't be extraordinarily amazing at everything (no matter how much we think we can), and we must all accept, if not embrace, our weaknesses. We previously talked about saying "Goodbye" to comfort and "Hello" to the willingness to fail. In this chapter, we want you to face your weaknesses, which may create discomfort initially, but it will allow you to apply your strengths in ways that make your weaknesses less significant to the outcome of your life. When we understand the nature of our pitfalls, we can then begin to develop and fine-tune our strengths as a weapon against our flaws. Whatever it is in life that you are not exactly great at, embrace it, acknowledge it, and work on it, because these weaknesses are a part of you. Do not let your flaws prevent you from reaching your goals and thwart your dreams. Instead, find ways to work with or improve on your shortcomings and push through the hard times.

Instead of getting caught up in the things in life that we struggle with, and telling ourselves and others that we are great at these issues, we must, instead, admit our flaws and work our backsides off to strengthen them. You might never completely turn a weakness into a strength *(after four years of statistics courses, I am still subpar, at best)*; however, you can improve and fine-tune your individual tools in order to combat these weak points, and sometimes, even master your weaknesses. If everything in life was easy, we would get bored very quickly. On a daily basis, men encounter hard work, challenges and struggles, which help to shape their lives and learn to be better people, all of which prevents them from becoming bored. I encourage you all to start working on your weaknesses. Don't be scared of them or hide them with lies and deceit. Embrace them, work on them, and soon enough, you will overcome these struggles. You may, in your area of weakness, be like me. I am not going to ever teach statistics, but I am not going to allow it to stop me from fulfilling my dreams either.

I want you to ask yourself how your father (or mentor) has helped you with your weaknesses. How does he deal with his own less than stellar characteristics? Has he shown an attitude of judgment or of gracious encouragement? In your work toward achieving manhood, it is important that the walls between you and your father come down. It may begin with each of you being man enough to apologize for what has gone wrong in your relationship and for the ways that you have disappointed one another. It takes tremendous courage for a son to be honest when telling his father how he has been disappointed by him. It takes great humility for a father to take responsibility for how he has disappointed his son. Only men are able to tolerate such honest feedback. You may not be ready to do this with each other yet, but as men, this is our goal. Jesus modeled this level of honest expression as He spoke the "truth in love." Eventually, we will all hurt those (of both genders) who are close to us or we will be hurt by them; however, what causes a relationship to grow as a result of these hurtful times is when each individual is man or woman enough to deal openly and directly with these disappointments.

Romans 14:4 states, "Who are you to judge someone else's servants? Whether they are faithful or not is their own master's concern. They will be faithful, because the Lord has the power to make them faithful." As you and your father take this journey together, it is important that you have the right spirit between you. There are many things in life that need to change, and that includes *you*. As we change, we must first deal with *what is* before we can deal with *what will be*. If there is judgment and a critical spirit within your relationship, you and your father will not be honest with each other, you will not seek forgiveness from each other, and growth will not occur. When these conversations occur, each man must give up his power, control, and condemnation; if each man does not, the whole process will be limited. My dad didn't judge me harshly regarding my struggles with math. As a result, we could deal honestly with *what is* so that I could get his assistance for *what should be.* God is the only judge who has the right to judge us. When observing Jesus' conversation with the woman at the well, He gave her the gift of *time.* Like the woman at the well, Jesus gives us this tremendous gift of time and He also gives us the time to change. As you and your father grow on this journey, give this gift of time to each other!

Manhood Discussion - Chapter 5

1. There is a difference between being able to look at your failures honestly and learning to accept that you have strengths and weaknesses. Identify one or more areas of weakness in your life. They may be related to school, your relationships, athletics, or some other area of life that you would like to be good at, but aren't.

2. What strengths do you have which can be used to surround your weak areas to maximize the positive parts of who you are?

3. How easy is it for you to talk to each other about the ways that each of you disappoint the other? Are you more likely to feel judged or accepted in these conversations?

4. Since being a man includes having a dream of what you want to be like in the future, share one or more dreams that you have for yourself. Share a dream you once had and whether or not you fulfilled it. Do you have any dreams for what your relationship with each other will be like?

5. Ephesians 4:15 states, "Instead, we will speak the truth in love. We will grow up into Christ in every way." What does this *Bible* verse mean in relation to the topic of this chapter?

Why Is It Important To Communicate And Why Does It Cost A Young Man When He Doesn't Communicate?

6

Research continues to show significant statistics regarding the fact that excellent communication skills increase the likelihood of being hired right out of college. Each year, more high schools and colleges are using group projects rather than individual assignments and presentations or papers in order to build these skills. In addition, they are stressing the importance of group cohesion and effective communication. When a political figure conveys an important message and completely botches it, we hurry to mock and belittle him for screwing up something so simple. Even our military has developed its own form of slang to ensure fast and reliable communication between soldiers during battle. Our nation understands how important communication is and does everything it can to start developing better communication patterns in our youth; we hold biases towards others regarding their communication styles, if it doesn't meet our standards. Then, why is it that the young men in today's society absolutely suck at communicating?

From the time that we learn to talk, until we graduate from high school or college, we are told, time and time again, how important communication is. As young boys, we are told not to use our fists, but to use words. As athletes, we are told that the key to success on the field is to communicate with our teammates. In the classroom, we are told to embrace group projects and presentations as a learning tool, as they are key to gaining entrance into the job field. For the first 22 years of my life I have been told how important communication is, but not once have I been told *why* it is important. Now, I'm sure there are a couple of you reading this book who think you are clever and say to yourselves, "Communication is important so that we can effectively exchange information with one another; this enables us to live a peaceful, productive, synchronized life in a world that allows us to gain and receive knowledge quicker, easier, and with greater understanding." Besides the fact that saying something like that would make you look like a peace-keeping, tree-hugging nerd, that comment still does not answer my question as to *why* communication is really that vital to a young man. Why is it that, for our first twenty-some years of life, we are told by everyone and "their uncle" how important communication is, but not a single person has ever stopped and taken the time to explain to us why communication is vital to a young man's well-being and growing maturity.

Tell a man there are a billion stars in the sky, and he will believe you. Tell him a bench has wet paint, he has to touch it to make sure. Men are hard-wired to be obedient, but also extremely curious, a dangerous combination, if you ask me. We are constantly pulled from opposite sides of the spectrum. We want to obey and please those who are in charge of us, but at the same time, we are continually driven to venture off and explore on our own, not giving two rips about what the group leaders will say when we return. While we are growing up, we are constantly getting into trouble as our curiosity gets the better of us, only to then find ourselves being scolded by a parent, teacher, coach, or other authority figure who tells us that we should have known better. From an early age we learn that the communication to a young man to sit down, shut up, and not fight back is frequent. The heck with our curiosity, we tell ourselves, and swear that we'll never step out of line again. As we tell ourselves this we are often in the middle of doing something inappropriate yet again, only to find ourselves back in the hot seat, once again being asked how we could be so stupid.

Our nation spends billions of dollars trying to solve the problems of our youth and each year more ideas are added in hopes of correcting our troubled kids. Instead of looking at each kid and determining which ones are destined to be problem children, allowing many of them to be victimized, and labeling the rest as perfect (which is not true), we should turn our attention to the adults. You see, kids are not super geniuses who, one day, wake up and learn words, string these words into sentences, sentences into paragraphs, and paragraphs into effective communication. They must be taught. And who are they taught by? Adults! I believe that when dealing with maturing young men, the adults who teach them have the opportunity to use their sword of knowledge by showing them the importance of effective communication. By doing so, these young men will one day be able to hold this great sword of knowledge and utilize what they have learned to benefit the next generation of men. Instead, these male adults end up cutting off their arm with their own sword as they fail to communicate with their children and adolescents appropriately. As young men, we are never taught the importance of having an equal relationship in the communication arena; instead, if we are told anything about communication, it involves sitting and listening, not voicing our opinions, and apologizing only to find ourselves repeating the offense all over again.

Many of our male role models are silent and talk only when they have to (which, more times than not, is when they are in trouble). We are taught to apologize, but not how to think in ways that lead to the good decisions which would prevent them from screwing up and needing to apologize again. Adults cannot fix a problem if they do not know the cause of the problem. Many young boys are spoken to in ways that prevent them from speaking up and sharing their thoughts about life with adults. This wall between young males and the adults who should teach them makes it impossible to figure out what is going on inside of our heads. Without this insight, they cannot help us. We are willing to sit and share with our close friends, as they do not judge us and scold us. However, when it comes to authority figures, we have come to the conclusion that judgment is everywhere and comes with a price. To become men, we need to talk, express ourselves appropriately, and at the same time, be strong enough to tolerate healthy levels of judgment and correction.

I find it rather funny when I hear our society complain that young children, and especially young boys, who are not communicating well, when it is our society that molds them into these less-than-wordsmith, C^+, childish males. We choose not to teach kids the importance of communication; we allow our kids to sit around for twenty-some years, then finally, when they are adults, we say to ourselves, "Crap – maybe we should have done more to teach them how to communicate with us." Instead of being proactive, we wait around until it is too late, complain a little, then give up on these so-called broken young males, telling ourselves that there is really no hope for getting them to communicate with us. The truth is, males will talk; however, they need to feel supported by the adults in their lives in order to do that. Often no one is there.

I am challenging the young men who are reading this book to start to perfect the art of communication. I understand that this challenge is a bit loaded because communication is a part of everything we do. From phone calls, text messaging, emails, and small talk to business meetings and group projects, and even the silence between two friends – all of these activities demonstrate the different types of communication that we participate in on a daily basis. Therefore, perfecting the art of communication is not something I expect you to accomplish in an hour. This concept might seem easy as you look around and see other men speaking with ease and whose communication has a great flow. However, you should be warned, these men are either wise and have had many years of practice, or they are bumbling idiots who use fancy words and snide comments to appear sophisticated.

There is no mathematical formula for turning less than wise young men into effective communication machines. However, I will tell you four pieces of manhood advice that can help you with this quest. First, as a man, the one which I am pretty sure that you will hate, is to read. If you are like me, you can not stand reading. You would much rather be outside slapping a stick against a rock or chasing the neighborhood cat around the block. This is not ingrained in our DNA, however. We have been taught as young men to hate reading. We are forced to read books for English class, that for the most part, are woman-friendly; they lack violence and interesting ideas and in general, put a growing boy to sleep rather quickly. I promise you that there are thousands of great books out there about plenty of manly topics that will not put you to sleep. Not only will you start to enjoy reading as I have learned to do, but it will make communicating, and communicating *properly*, that much easier for you.

31

The second thing that you must do to help yourself improve your verbal skills is to surround yourself with Bull Elephants. These men know how to get their point across; they listen to what others have to say, and rarely get aggravated when they are in an argument or in the midst of a discussion. These men understand that being able to verbalize their feelings and emotions, along with being able to understand another person's emotions during a conversation, helps them to effectively communicate in all settings. Whether in a business meeting, talking with a friend, or in a rather intense discussion, they understand how to exchange words with another person in order to steer the conversation in the direction that they want, using a calm voice, unwavering courage, and a patient disposition.

The third piece of advice that I have for you is one that, once you start, you will never stop working on. Push yourself. Some men decide that reading is not for them and eventually, we all must step out from under the wings of our Bulls. This step is one that every man can continue to practice and fine-tune until the day he dies. Do not be afraid of approaching a conversation that is difficult or challenging. Stand firm when you are facing trouble and hold your core values close when you are in the midst of tough arguments. Do not be afraid of hearing an outcome that you are not exactly fond of. You must understand that we do not always get sunshine and roses in this life, and more times than not, it is just a bunch of malarkey. A true man needs to understand the importance of receiving information that he is not exactly thrilled with, taking it in, digesting it, remaining calm, and then using it as fuel to drive him toward becoming a better person.

Would you rather appear right *or* be smart? You can't have both. Lastly, I advise you to share your thoughts because it is the only way to discover distortions in your thinking; we need to show humility when discovering our flaws, and use all of this to refine our perspective. You must have strength and confidence in the fact that you have value even when you don't know everything. You must want to be wise more than you care about how you appear to others. The truth is, most of us aren't that good looking anyhow! Therefore, it is best to emphasize that you want to learn as much as possible and take risks by sharing how you think with others.

Have you ever had a conversation with a five-year old? A kid can ramble on for hours about every single detail of the day and launch off into a million and a half tangents about completely irrelevant things. You sit there patiently and wait for the story to end before you grow old and die. Now, take this same five-year old and add a few years to his life. As a teenager he is still inherently the same person; however, you can't get a word out of him. He sits there in silence, lacking most, if not all, basic social skills. Why is this? How did the five-year old who didn't know when to shut up turn into the teenage boy who hardly talks at all? At some point, this young boy started hearing worries from that whispering voice in his head. This voice started telling him how to dress, talk, walk, and everything in between. It also told him that everyone was looking at him all the time, and if he didn't want to embarrass himself, he should listen very carefully and not say anything stupid.

Fathers, I encourage you to be really conscious of the social skills that your son needs to learn. You need to understand and accept that a young man's early teenage years to his early twenties are an extremely difficult time. There is a constant struggle within him between that whisper in his head which is telling him that he is embarrassing himself, and his true self, which is telling him that he must stand up for himself and say what he thinks.

Good communication is often difficult, embarrassing, tough, challenging, and anything but fun. However, it is these challenging conversations that we all must have which will help us grow and develop into strong young men. If we are Christians, we seek God's input in our conversations because we know that when we talk we represent Him. This is a significant responsibility that we carry. We also look to God to provide us with guidance and answers as a result of our conversations with Him. But, we must also understand that, sometimes, the answers that we are searching for or asking about are not clearly visible. The Lord speaks in a still small voice; a voice that is often overlooked if we are actively searching for direct answers from God. When someone prays for patience, they expect a gift-wrapped package filled with patience that can be used whenever it is needed. However, God works in mysterious ways that are hard for us to imagine. Instead of granting us patience like a magic genie, He gives us the *opportunity* to practice being patient. Do you see the difference?

As members of the Give-Me-Nation, we have a difficult time listening and waiting. We would rather have someone give us immediate solutions without an explanation of how or why. God is a phenomenal listener and a wise one, at that. He offers opportunities to practice important life skills rather than simply instilling the particular attribute that we ask Him for. This helps us grow as individuals and helps us learn the importance of certain life skills.

The best way for us to learn how to communicate well with others is to talk with God more. This helps us to know God at deeper levels, which also helps us understand ourselves better, all of which God wants. 1 Thessalonians 5:17 states, "Never stop praying." This doesn't mean that we constantly talk about what we *want* and need from God because, if we did, we would run out of things on our request list or become bored with its repetition. More importantly, if you are a young man like me who is striving for manhood, you feel guilty about asking others constantly for help and guidance while never offering anything in return. By becoming aware of these conversations and increasing their frequency, we can start to hear ourselves talk. As God helps us change our internal self-talk by conversing with Him regularly, our communication skills grow. Because of their miraculous nature, moment-by-moment conversations with God keep us fresh. On some level, God will always be mysterious, and His actions and conversations are never "predictable." Praying regularly can help you become more aware of how you communicate, which will also improve your communication with others.

When faced with a challenging life situation, you must first understand that the use of communication can solve a lot of your worries, problems, and questions. By communicating your feelings and listening to others, you will find that your biggest worry is often far from the actual outcome of a situation. I encourage each of you to start looking at your conversations with others, similarly to how you would listen to the Word of God. Sometimes, if not most times, people can't give you a direct answer nor can they give you the answer you are looking for. Rather than brushing them off and treating what they had to say as a waste of time, look at the conversation as a gift or an opportunity to grow.

Manhood Discussion - Chapter 6

1. Do you see yourself as a good communicator or bad one? What areas of life are easiest for you to talk about? Which areas of life are hard for you to talk about? Is it harder for you to talk about external issues or internal issues?

2. Identify three questions that you have about life. Regardless of whether you like school or not, are you aware of the instinct within you that likes to learn and is curious? How easy is it for you to tell someone that you are sorry and apologize?

3. Identify several situations (or people) where you are most likely to feel judged. Identify several situations (or people) where you are most likely to feel accepted. Are you more likely to be seen by others as a judgmental person or an accepting person? What type of behavior(s) are you automatically judgmental of because you define it as wrong?

4. Discuss whether it is difficult for you to enjoy reading. What topics or issues do you like to read about? How aware are you of the constant conversations that are going on inside your head?

5. Apply the *Bible* verse, "Never stop praying" (1 Thessalonians 5:17) to your discussion of this chapter.

The Bulls At Bloomsburg

I'll admit, I might have been one of the few graduating seniors who was not ready to leave college. I was holding on to every minute of my last few weeks there, hoping to suck just a little more knowledge out of my classes and the library, secretly telling myself to fail a class so that I could go back for another year. I was blessed to be part of the psychology program at Bloomsburg University. The professors in the psychology department did not just lecture their students, but understood (as all psychologists do) that we weren't just students, but people, and more importantly, individuals. Each professor approached their students as individuals and made an effort to get to know us on more than just a student-teacher basis. They wanted to get to know us on a deeper level and wanted us to get to know them as well.

I will share with you about two Bull Elephants who crossed my path during my studies at Bloomsburg University. These two men taught me more than just psychology. They taught me manhood. I have tremendous respect for these two gentlemen and thank them for helping me through some of the difficult times I experienced while transitioning from adolescence into adulthood. Both men have my respect; they both deserve to have their wisdom passed on to my readers. As the knowledge and wisdom of both of them is irreplaceable and extremely valuable in its own right, I cannot possibly rank knowledge of one as more important than the other. With this, I want my readers to understand that the order of these stories means nothing. As a psychology major, I will do what I have always been taught and put my sources in alphabetical order *(see, I picked up at least one thing at college).* One last side note – not only are these two men Bull Elephants, but they both, in their own ways, look quite like Bull Elephants.

I worked under Dr. Beck as a Teacher's Assistant for his general psychology courses during my senior year at college. While working with Dr. Beck, I saw what a great man he was, as I was able to get to know him on a deeper level than a teacher-student relationship. I saw the passion that this man had for teaching and decided to take his clinical psychology course during my final semester. I strolled into Dr. Beck's class ready to learn about all the exciting adventures clinical psychology had to offer. After all, I was already certain that I wanted to become a licensed clinical psychologist after I obtain my Doctorate degree of psychology (Psy.D.) a few years down the road. I can honestly say, even a few short weeks after his class, I didn't retain one piece of information about clinical psychology (sorry Dr. Beck). However, what I did learn, was much, *much* more useful, not only as a future psychologist, but as a man.

Dr. Beck taught me how to "*suck it up.*" Pretty straight forward, right? This man taught me how to battle through life's struggles and press on in the face of hard times. Here was a guy who taught in Pennsylvania and lived in Florida. He would fly back and forth every week in order to spend weekends with his family. In addition, he was struggling with a few health issues, while at the same time dealing with the hassle of airports on a weekly basis. To top it off, he was dealing with the declining health of his father, and would periodically need to leave Bloomsburg, at a moment's notice, and fly to Florida when his father would take a turn for the worse, only to fly back a few days later and continue teaching, as if nothing happened. Not once, did this man ever let any of this affect his attitude. He came barging into class each day, smiling and laughing, asking students about *their* problems, and downright sucking it up every dang day. You see, men deal with struggles every day, all day. But, it is those who know how to deal with their pain, press through hard times, and have a positive outlook on life who make it through the sludge. Males who choose to hang on to their struggles, adopt an attitude that life is out to get them, and convince themselves that they always have the "short end of the stick," get caught up in the negative parts of life. Eventually, they crash and burn.

Yes, Dr. Beck owes a lot of his high morale to his wife and family for their great support, but what it really comes down to is this man's testicular fortitude. He understood the amount of respect his students had for him and wanted to make sure he was always at the top of his game. On a more personal level, Dr. Beck was great at making *me* suck it up. He held me to high standards and entrusted me with helping out when he couldn't make it to class. One day, I received an email from him telling me quite simply to *suck it up*. We had an assignment due for class that was to be initiated via email. I could rattle off 1,007 other issues that I had going on in my life as excuses for not turning in the assignment on time. However, this brilliant man knew I was also striving to be a man and not merely a male. He was not going to settle for my subpar performance and let me know it. With clear and direct words of encouragement, he snapped me back into place rather quickly. I handed in the assignment late, apologized for my shortcomings, and fessed up to my slippage into maleness. I wasn't expecting to receive credit for my late assignment and did not go to his office to beg him to let this issue slide by, just this once. I went to him and apologized because that is what men do. I held him to high standards as a Bull Elephant and knew he held me to high standards as a young man. He should expect nothing less. I still have his email to me as a reminder that excuses are the nails in a house of failure.

Dr. Tloczynski, or Dr. T as he is referred to around Bloomsburg, was my Independent Study advisor on the topic of religious orientation and college adjustment and taught Psychology Seminar: Spirituality and Religiosity. Here was a man with a deep and solid belief in God teaching very controversial subjects to a group of impressionable students; he not only taught extremely well, but taught with a purpose. He was an excellent teacher when teaching his actual subject matter, but also when teaching core values, honesty, and integrity. He would urge us to immerse ourselves in our reaction papers, and not just give summaries of the many books that we read for class. He would press us to dig deeper and to challenge ourselves to really search our hearts for answers, not to just rely on the easy answers.

One day during class, Dr. T gave us a brief lecture on meditation and the benefits it brings to maintaining a healthy lifestyle. He took us through the steps involved in meditation and let us practice meditating for about 15 minutes. The actual demonstration is not the point I am driving at; I am also not telling all of you to go out and buy books on meditation and start this practice. My point is, your mind needs exercise, just like your body.

At some point in most, if not every young man's life, he decides that it is time to ditch his tiny, feeble, weakling body, pick up some weights, and transform himself into a hardened Spartan Warrior. He quickly notices progress and thoroughly enjoys the aesthetic pleasure that comes with weight-lifting. As human beings, we are very visual creatures, so when a young boy starts to lift weights and can actually see the progress he is making, he becomes completely ecstatic with his results. What Dr. T taught me is that your brain (or mind) is a muscle too. The mind, just like every other muscle in your body, must be trained and exercised in order to grow. Without the right kinds of exercise, a muscle will not grow and we will be weaker than those around us who are training hard.

So, why is it that mastering the art of meditation is so difficult? Because we are visual creatures! We can't physically *see* the progress we are making with meditation (or any form of growth with our mind). When we can't physically see our progress, we feel as if nothing is happening and give up rather quickly. Dr. T instilled in me the notion of working on things in my life that I cannot physically see. He taught me the importance of determination and commitment to the growth of my mind and other parts of me that are unseen. It is extremely difficult to remain committed to something when we cannot see its benefits or any external display of our hard work. For this reason, many males give up on the quest for knowledge and the search for truth. Manhood means that you must buckle down and do what is needed to grow mentally and spiritually. Did you know that the biggest and strongest muscle in the Bull Elephant is his mind?!

Dr. T was also a great mentor for teaching me the art of acceptance. Beginning in middle school, young boys start to think that the entire globe is watching every move they make. If we want to be popular and fit in, we think we need to be careful about every move we make and only do things that won't put our reputation in jeopardy. Dr. T showed me that, in the end, it really does not matter what others think. He showed the power and truth found in the Serenity Prayer in his life: "Lord, grant me the serenity to accept the things I cannot change, the courage to change the things I can, and the wisdom to know the difference." If a girl breaks up with you – so what? That simply means she wasn't the right one for you. You are just wasting your time and energy trying to convince her and yourself that the two of you belong together. When it comes to impressing others, you really don't need to do much. If you just act like yourself, be yourself, and do things that you have always been doing, those who are like-minded and have the same mindset as you will find you. So, instead of wasting our time worrying about what everyone else thinks, let us take a step back and accept what is. Be yourself while you work on becoming a man and those real friends, who will enjoy you for who you are, will find you.

Both of these Bulls saw that what is not easily seen in life is much more significant than what is seen. They supported my growth, not just on an external level, but by emphasizing what was going on inside of me as well. They taught me to get ready to affect life by making a difference, while accepting what "is," at the same time. John 4:24 states, "God is Spirit. His worshipers must worship him in spirit and in truth." There are many ways that we, as young men, can be tempted to see life simplistically, in a concrete way. Whether or not we choose to recognize the spiritual world that is beneath all we see, it is still there. It benefits a man to take a step back from his busy lifestyle, from his daily grind, from the hustle and bustle of the work week, and develop and reflect on his spiritual self. It is easy not to put this time aside, but if we don't, we will find ourselves walking aimlessly through life and accomplishing little of importance. Understanding our priorities and achieving our goals demands that we look at God, who is *not* seen and place Him higher than what is seen.

Manhood Discussion - Chapter 7

1. Dad: Share with your son what you hope he will learn from observing you. Identify a couple of mistakes that you have made which you hope that he doesn't repeat. Why? Son: Identify something that you have learned from your dad. If you became a dad in the future, what would you hope your son would learn from you?

2. Son: Identify a time when your Dad said, "Suck it up!" and you knew he was right. Identify a time when your Dad disciplined you and you knew it was right for him to correct you. What level of importance do each of you give to the use of excuses? Are excuses the behavior of a male or a man?

3. How comfortable are you with the act of meditating or taking time to reflect on how you are doing in life? Identify a quiet place where you feel safe and can spend time alone with yourself and God. Do you agree with Dr. T that the brain is a muscle that should be exercised?

4. Identify several aspects of your invisible world (either inside of you or outside of you). The "Serenity Prayer" states: "Lord grant me the serenity to accept the things I cannot change; the courage to change the things I can; and the wisdom to know the difference." How easy is it for you to believe and practice what this prayer states? What do you need to change? Is this a change you can make? What do you need to accept about your life?

5. Ephesians 6:12 states, "Our fight is not against human beings. It is against the rulers, the authorities and the powers of this dark world. It is against the spiritual forces of evil in the heavenly world." Apply this *Bible* verse to your discussion of this chapter.

Prove It, My Friend

8

"Dad, some kid at school said that eagles can stay airborne for up to 90 years!" There were countless pieces of information that I would bring home to my dad and share, only for him to chuckle and ask me what kind of proof there was for this latest "fact." I would always offer a rebuttal by telling him the tidbit had to be true because this kid's brother's dog walker's sister's hair dresser's landlord said it, and he was a very reputable guy. He would take me to the computer and start researching the latest piece of information with me, showing me that it is impossible for an eagle to stay airborne for 90 years, as the average lifespan is only 20 years. Through years of rebuttal, my father taught me the important characteristic of being a skeptic. You see, being a skeptic is a very strong quality of a Christian man. He understands that there are many falsehoods in life, and that if he is to accept all facts as truth, he runs the risk of falling victim to the unwise. A wise person is one who listens to all sides and accepts the more credible side as being the greater truth. Instead of blindly accepting everything anyone has ever told us, we must constantly search for truth. By being individuals who are constantly searching for honesty, we are truly being men. A man grows wise by searching for truth. He then shares these truths with those who will listen, in hope of leading them toward knowledge in ways similar to what he has done himself.

The choice to be skeptical, and not to immediately accept everything you hear as credible, can produce several outcomes. First, you internally become a stronger man. You understand that by carefully listening and sifting through the "malarkey" to find truth, you are gaining wisdom and knowledge. You are beginning to say "Goodbye" to your previous dependency by taking responsibility for developing your own beliefs. On an external level, you start to show others that you are, in fact, a knowledgeable man. Knowledge produces credibility and once others decide that you are credible, they begin to listen to your words of wisdom. My hope is that all of you become a little more skeptical and start searching for truth. With this, you will be able to help others as my father has helped me, and be a beacon of truth for those who are lost at sea. In fact, you can start by being skeptical of my advice about skepticism! Don't just accept what I am saying, but instead push yourself to the point of straining, to find the truth in my words of advice. Until you personalize anything you hear by doing the hard work of looking at it skeptically, what you think or believe will not be solid. As youngsters, it is challenging to deal with the world. The process of skepticism which leads to stronger beliefs is what is necessary to deal with life's next attacks.

Part of being a knowledgeable man means not succumbing to the majority rule and standing your ground when faced with a group of others who completely disagree with you. It is easy to stray from your beliefs when faced with a group of others who claim that you are wrong. During my final semester at Bloomsburg, I was enrolled in an upper level Psychology Seminar course that focused on the topic of spirituality and religiosity. This was a very controversial class that produced many arguments and some ill feelings between classmates. The class, as a whole, was mostly agnostic or atheistic, and the kids who were Christians were more or less confused in their faith. Every day was an uphill battle for me as I tried to convince my fellow students that Christ was our true Savior and that He was our ticket to an afterlife. This class was a perfect example of the value of being skeptical, and thus becoming wise and able to stand firm in the face of opposition.

There was a particular student in class who was certain there could be no God and that I was foolish for my beliefs. At the beginning of the semester he had the class convinced that he was a genius and that what I had to say was nothing more than psychotic. I could have given up and succumbed to the group norms, but instead I fought through it and held firm in my beliefs. I cannot attest to what the other students believed towards the end of class when it came to their faith and the existence of God, but what I can tell you is this: Every day, more kids would tell me that whether or not there was a God, my arguments *for* Christ began to be seen as more authentic, legitimate, and wise. What they saw as genius in my opponent at first now seemed farfetched, idiotic, and immature. By listening to my father's advice and being skeptical, I was able to see through my opponent's remarks and help my classmates towards the greater truth. What is even more significant, however, is that I took responsibility, as a young man, to establish my beliefs. Establishing strength in what you believe is not an accident. It comes with hard work and mental toughness.

Part of the time that you spend with your father should be used to challenge each other to provide backup (or proof) for the opinions each of you have. Proverbs 27:17 states, "As iron sharpens iron, so one person sharpens another." The strength of each man's viewpoints must be tested. This will inherently cause sparks between the two of you; however, instead of coming to a standstill, you both should be allowed to ask the simple question, "Why do you think that?"

Fathers, remember that many times, the authority figures in a young boy's life have taught him to sit down and be quiet. He is told time after time that he should never question the authorities in his life. Teach him that it is okay to ask *why*; as your son begins to ask you questions about life, you are helping him grow up to be a man. My father encouraged me to disagree and to question, saying that he never wanted me to be a clone: "I will have failed if you agree with everything I say and if you believe everything I believe."

When dealing with these questions, fathers must keep in mind that this father-son (mentor-mentee) relationship is not exactly an equal relationship. In this way, the father (or mentor) should remember to act as Jesus said, "And those who are first will be last" (Matthew 20:16). Jesus expected this of himself, as well as His disciples. He wanted them to learn to sacrifice for each other. In your relationship, the person with less authority should decide who goes first and should also be allowed to control the time they spend together. The safer your son feels, the more progress he will make toward becoming a man.

As we watch Jesus' life with his disciples, we see the graciousness he showed them as he taught them. When Peter overstepped the line and told Jesus how he should think, Jesus confronted him (Matthew 16:22-23). Each person in this manhood journey should be allowed to speak his opinion and those opinions should be respected. Telling another man what to think and how he should act results in anger and hostility. When Jesus met Saint Thomas, a man known as "Doubting Thomas," Jesus didn't have a problem with his questions. Instead, he helped him solidify his beliefs by dealing directly with his skepticism. Thomas, as a result of being able to freely express his questions, became willing to die for his faith. Since our goal is to grow in our manhood, any honest question should be seen as helping us to reach our goal.

Manhood Discussion - Chapter 8

1. Allow yourself some time to enjoy this question. Share some thoughts or ideas that you once thought were true and have since learned are not. Spending time thinking is part of growing up and becoming a man. As we learn to think, our thoughts and opinions may change as more facts come in. Learning to accept this process helps us to be humble about what we know.

2. Identify three important questions for which you are both seeking answers. How would you answer the other person's question if you had asked the same question yourself?

3. Discuss the concept that mental toughness is created by being skeptical and having the courage, energy, and perseverance to seek answers. Do you agree that each man must answer the following questions for himself: Is there a God? How should I relate to this God?

4. How difficult is it for you not to break the social-skill rule about telling another person how to think? Do you agree that the power struggle that occurs when this rule is broken hurts a person's ability to personalize their own beliefs? Do you think that it is the parent's responsibility to teach their son how to act until he is independent and responsible for himself?

5. Acts 17:11 states, "The Bereans were very glad to receive Paul's message. They studied the Scriptures carefully every day. They wanted to see if what Paul said was true. So they were more noble than the Thessalonians." How does this *Bible* verse relate to the topic of this chapter?

I Have Become All Things To All People So That By All Possible Means I Might Save Some

During the beginning stages of writing this book, I would spend many hours in my mentor's office discussing what should be included, what should be omitted, how to go about certain topics and the overall "feel" of the book. (My mentor is very close to my family and me, and is a man I consider to be not only a Bull Elephant, but an "uncle.") I would send him the rough draft of what I had written so far, he would read over it, and we would discuss it. During one particular meeting, Uncle Roy shared a story with me that I will pass on to you. Around the time that my parents were getting married, he was invited along with my parents to dinner at my grandparent's house. My grandparents are extremely traditional and devoted their lives to being missionaries. My uncle, on the other hand, is … well … a trucker at heart. This man, in his younger years, could string together words that would make even the roughest pirate's ears explode. My parents were convinced that my uncle could not last through an entire dinner conversation with my mother's conservative parents without dropping a few unacceptable words. My uncle made it through the entire dinner and proved everyone wrong.

Since my uncle has become ordained, has matured, or has gotten too old, his trucker side has mellowed and his language has become much more boring. He has cut down on his "pirate lingo" by about 95%. Imagine my surprise when this once-trucker talker turned the subject of the conversation to *my* language *(that was the pot calling the kettle black if you ask me)*. He continued by explaining to me that we could proceed in writing the

47

book in its original form or we could tone down the expressive language in it and find different words to replace certain words. He finalized his speech with a quote from Paul, a follower of Jesus,

> I am free. I don't belong to anyone. But I make myself a slave to everyone. I do it to win as many as I can to Christ. To the Jews I became like a Jew. That was to win the Jews. To those under the law I became like one who was under the law, even though I myself am not under the law. That was to win those under the law. To those who don't have the law I became like one who doesn't have the law. I am not free from God's law. I am under Christ's law. Now I can win those who don't have the law. To those who are weak I became weak. That was to win the weak. I have become all things to all people so that in all possible ways I might save some. I do all of that because of the good news. And I want to share in its blessings. (1 Corinthians 9:19-23)

You see, whether or not one is a Christian, in order to become a man, he must live his life as Paul did. My uncle encouraged me to keep a bit of a muzzle on my less than creative use of language in hope of becoming all things to all people *or*, in other words, to reach out to more. I could have published this book using some street language and touched the lives of a very specific group. Or I could use a thesaurus, and work harder at expressing myself differently. Since I don't know you I must be careful, because your relationship with God is more important than not being careful with my tongue. I may have a different view about this issue than you, but God says offending others should only occur by speaking His truth.

Instead of reaching out to some and offending the rest, I decided to put a cap on how I sometimes express myself and use what I believe to be less flamboyant language (*polite may be a word some of you would use*). However, by putting a halt to my "brilliant" vocabulary I am able to become all things to all people, thus reaching out to more. So, as I have tried very hard to do this, and I believe I have succeeded (at least for the most part), I encourage you all to try as well. There are many times in life when we feel it is too difficult, too time consuming, or just down right too annoying to reach out to more people rather than less. However, as a male growing toward manhood, you must understand that choosing the easy route is something that every man must battle.

To apply this philosophical and theological issue to a more modern day understanding, I will correlate what Paul did to a concept that my friends and I used in high school. If two of us were to ever get in an argument, eventually one would claim that he was going to be "the bigger man and step down." Now, this was used as a direct insult as he was indirectly telling his verbal adversary that he was a better person by dropping the argument and letting the matter go. Oddly enough, even though we had the wrong motivation for such "bigger" man statements, we might have been on to something; as the concept is something we can all use. Rather than holding a grudge, huffing and puffing, and becoming angry with others, we can simply make a choice to be the bigger man. Instead of moaning about how I have to watch my use of language so that I don't insult someone, I can accept that life isn't always about what I want; if I truly want to help as many people as I can, I must be all things to all people *or* be the bigger man.

The *concept* of being the bigger man is a very straightforward and easy one to talk about or write down on paper. However, be warned, the use of this concept on a daily basis is very difficult to master. Failure will occur. By telling ourselves or others that we are better than someone else because we are doing or not doing something in order to please them, or to avoid offending them, is to misuse what Saint Paul meant. Instead, we are, in reality, telling everyone around us that we are actually an immature man! Becoming a man takes a lot of self-discipline and patience. There is a difference between bragging to those who will listen to how much of a man we are, while we wear our manhood on our sleeves, as opposed to doing what is right. If we are true men, they will be witnesses to our deeds; they will not have to hear about our manly choices from us. Be careful, as there is a very fine line between claiming that we have achieved manhood and actually walking the difficult path of manhood on a daily basis. The presence of humility is the easiest way to show whether we are on a male path or a manhood journey. Instead of strutting, we must do what it says in Matthew 5:16: "In the same way, let your life shine in front of others. Then will they see the good things you do. And they will praise your Father who is in heaven."

Saint Paul said, "I have become all things to all people so that in all possible ways I might save some" (1 Corinthians 9:22). We want to explain this concept through a psychological perspective with the hope of making it a bit clearer. Back in the early 20th century, the psychoanalytic approach more or less dominated the field of psychology. Sigmund Freud, known as the founding father of psychoanalysis, along with his followers, felt that diagnosis and treatment was done through the careful observation of the subconscious of the client. The psychoanalytic approach utilized the psychologist's expertise to determine the client's issues. The approach to each client was the same: The client would come in and be diagnosed just like the previous patient and then was taught how to correct his/her mistakes in order to start living a happier, successful lifestyle. This approach treats each person assuming they are more similar to each other than they are different.

However, in the 1940s, a new branch of psychology started to emerge, called phenomenology. Starting with Carl Rogers, known for his development of client-centered therapy, introduced a whole new approach of dealing with clients. Instead of seeing clients as mindless drones who came in seeking help from experts, Rogers and his followers understood that each person was unique. Phenomenologists were not interested in putting people in a box with a diagnosis which specified the exact treatment of their disorder; instead, they were interested in helping the client work internally through their specific struggles. This approach was a client-centered approach; it meant that they saw each patient as a unique individual, rather than clumping them into a specific category of mental disorders.

To make this phenomenological approach a bit clearer, I will explain the concept of qualia. Qualia (or quale) is a term used to give anything perceived by our five senses an independent structure or definition, so that we can distinguish it from objects similar to it. Every sense in this world is or has qualia: the qualia of red for example, or the taste of orange juice after brushing your teeth. However, who is to say that you and I share the same taste when drinking orange juice after brushing our teeth? Yes, we both make the same disgusted look as we taste it. We might even agree that it is a very pungent, sour, and overall gross taste. But how can we be certain that you and I are experiencing the exact same taste after drinking the same thing? The phenomenological approach understood that, as humans, we are individuals and as individuals, we are unique. These thinkers did not try and clump their patients into categories, but instead, realized that each person was unique and helped each client with their specific needs.

You see, these men who took a phenomenological approach, or a client-centered approach, were following the idea of becoming all things to all people. Rather than treating every client the same and following the typical psychological guidelines for their diagnosis, they saw each client as an individual and helped them work through their problems in ways that were unique to who they were. By focusing each client's session in a unique manner that was geared toward the client rather than the therapist, these psychologists approached every client by becoming all things to all people, with the goal of saving some.

What was the result of this change to the way people who sought help were viewed? They got better. The power of respecting each individual, combined with the recognition that each person is different, empowered them to change the negative ways that they were feeling and acting. They no longer had to feel stuck in their negative ruts because they began to see themselves in a more positive light, which motivated them to be more optimistic. Jesus demonstrated His respect of others by how He spent His time with them. Whoever He was with, He saw value in them, despite the status given to them by their culture. By treating them in this way, these people who were once identified as "losers" were able to become the powerful disciples of Jesus and helped change the world. Just imagine if Jesus had taken the psychoanalytic approach and treated all of His disciples the same way. By ignoring their differences, He would have seen Peter as having the same negative potential as Judas. Instead, He saw each one's specific needs and gifts. He heard each of them individually and met them where they were at. He adjusted His interventions in their lives to match their particular personality style and needs.

In Romans 14, the *Bible* talks about the ways that we, as Christians, disagree with each other regarding what is right or wrong. We have hurt Christ's cause by becoming so distracted by these minor issues that we fail to love our brothers and sisters in Christ. People have varying needs regarding the level of structure that is required to support and maintain their faith. The *Bible* asks us not to judge others or look down on someone who has a rule that we do not. "Now then, who are you to judge your brother or sister? Why do you look down on them? We will all stand in God's courtroom to be judged. … So we will all have to explain to God the things we have done" (Romans 14:10-12). It is never a good idea to focus on the faults of others; rather, we need to act with thoughtfulness in our interactions with everyone.

Manhood Discussion - Chapter 9

1. Is there someone who has offended you? What did they do to offend you? Identify someone you have offended and how. How important is it to you not to offend another person?

2. How do you feel about the concept of the "bigger man" taking the initiative to start an interaction that improves the relationship? Identify several choices that you have made in a specific situation that required you to step up and be the bigger man.

3. How difficult is it for you to listen to other people? It is natural for us to believe that we know someone better than they know themselves. How do you stop yourself from being judgmental of others? How do you deal with the people in your life who judge you?

4. Discuss the ways that our society categorizes people. Identify the ways that you categorize people. Have you ever been put in a category and because of it, been treated negatively? What do you think about prejudice? Where do you see it happening around you? How did Jesus deal with people who were judgmental?

5. Matthew 5:16 states, "In the same way, let your light shine in front of others. Then they will see the good things you do. And they will praise your Father who is in heaven." Apply this *Bible* verse to your discussion of this chapter.

The Art Of Being Authentic

This chapter will piggyback on the previous chapter because we need to balance being all things to all people while also being authentic. If you have ever watched any of the television shows revolving around pawn shops, you will see people bringing in artifacts and items which they believe are real, only to be informed by an expert that what they have is a copy or a fake and not actually authentic. This holds true for males who have avoided the hard work of manhood. They are unaware of what they believe, and because of this, they go along with any influence that comes their way. They lack the internal character structure that is needed to make decisions that are consistent with the way they should live. They change their behavior, based on the circumstances they are in. They are unreliable because they change their position at a moment's notice when it is inconvenient to be ethical and consistent. The emptiness that they feel inside leads to an unsatisfying existence because they never know who they truly are.

Now, let's take a trip to my grandmother's house, a lady I love dearly and have the greatest respect for. When I am with her, it never crosses my mind to speak the same way to her as I would to my friends. My grandmother would be offended and hurt if she heard me talking about issues the way I do with my peers. My friends and I are different from her. As Christians working on our manhood, we must understand that it is unacceptable to hurt someone else. To violate her ideas of what life is would be to care about myself more than I care about her. If I am truly a man, I can be authentic and loving, no matter what circumstance I'm in. My self-expression changes to fit her style. I'm still authentic because my love for her causes me to choose to not emphasize our differences. I act this way because I have made a conscious choice to do this. It fits with my character to place her above myself in this way. I haven't lost myself as a male would, and I've become stronger by following my values which are to respect her.

True men have one self – their *authentic self*. They understand that we as men, beginning with Adam, have decided to become our own gods and overthrow the real God. When we did this, our imperfections became permanent. Men are opinionated and have beliefs that contradict the viewpoints of others. We all have different strengths, weaknesses, and perspectives. A true man understands this. When a man takes the time to understand the differing views of others, he is authentic. He makes certain not to offend others unless there is a specific God-given reason to do so. Jesus taught us some revolutionary and unique concepts. He knows that if we live for him, we will offend those who choose values that don't match our Christian values. I believe that if a man spends his life being all things to all people, and does this while being authentic, he has created the balance that manhood demands. In the end, you are hurting others as well as yourself, when you are being unauthentic or needlessly offensive.

Did you ever know a kid who appeared, at first, to be authentic, but who you quickly discovered was the complete opposite? We'll call this type of guy Unauthentic Joe *(sorry to you real Joe's out there)*. Unauthentic Joe is the type of kid who *appears* to back you up if you happen to find your-self in an argument with someone. He is likely to amp you up and tell you that you have the right to be mad, and that your opponent knows nothing and you should fight back. He basically has a you "go get 'em" approach. Unfortunately, behind your back, Unauthentic Joe will be tell-ing your opponent the exact same thing. You see, this type of weak male wants everyone's approval; he wants to be an important friend to you, as well as to them. He wants you to admire him and make him important by keeping him in the center of things. He is willing to create and use conflict to make himself powerful and liked by all. The effect is that conflict surrounds this type of male; he uses a cheap form of temporary social power, and eventually burns the friendship bridges he has with those around him. You can spot this type of unauthentic male by the controversy which surrounds him, and it would be best for you to keep your distance from him.

It is only a matter of time before Unauthentic Joe will notice that other people are staying away from him. He *appears* to be all things to all people, but his lack of authenticity doesn't support it. His opinions are soon disregarded, and he is gradually shifted out of any group of friends. Over time, people like him repeat this same pattern over and over again; unless they change, they will eventually lose their close friends. Unauthentic Joe's strategy for gaining acceptance from others is flawed. We must not be unauthentic by gossiping and using our power to create conflict in our relationships with others. If we live for ourselves in this way, we are not becoming all things to all people; we are simply using them. To sell out what we stand for is to put our manhood on hold. Men do what is tough by not using others and by not compromising their principles. As men, we must balance authenticity with becoming all things to all people.

Matthew 10:34 states, "Do not think that I came to bring peace to the earth. I didn't come to bring peace. I came to bring a sword." God makes it clear that He has called us, as men, to fight for truth. Sometimes, this will mean that we offend those who are wrong. Other times, we must be the "bigger" man and adjust our actions, so that we don't hurt someone. Authenticity demands that we make this kind of choice on a regular basis. Yes, at first, your unauthentic ways may fool others, lead them to trust you, and give you some form of popularity. However, sooner or later, others will see your true self and you'll end up alone. Be authentic, because your true colors will be found out!

My high school soccer coach didn't teach me a whole lot either on or off the field. However, there was one piece of advice he would give our team every year that I feel applies directly to authenticity. Before every season started, he would explain to us that because of the popularity of our team, we had a bit of a target on our backs. Some people would be looking for ways to get the members of our team in trouble. He would explain to us that you can do 100 things right or 1,000 things right, and if you get just one thing wrong, people will remember you for what you did wrong. So, for those of us who are striving to become men, we must understand that we, too, have a target on our backs. Our enemies, both spiritual and human, will see us working hard at becoming a better person and will do everything they can to stop our growth process. They will be constantly watching, hoping, wishing, and waiting for us to screw up, just once. They don't want us to succeed when they, themselves, aren't willing to pay the manhood price. At the same time, our friends and loved ones will be watching too, supporting our growth. Let's be real men, and stay balanced in our interactions with others. We need to control ourselves and not let who we are be up for a vote.

With everyone's eyes fixed on us, we must understand how important it is to be our authentic self. We could maybe get away with hiding our true (bad) colors a hundred times, but really, what good would it be? Everything around us would be unreal, because we would have made it that way. And then, if someone were to say they loved us, we wouldn't be able to tell what part of us they truly loved if we had chosen to fool them and hide our true self. When we put our beliefs aside and act in distorted and unauthentic ways to others, we are the ones being hurt.

Being a man is a challenge in a world that lacks authenticity. When you stand for something, it will create tension in your environment. You must be tough, as well as committed to following God's way in order to withstand the pressure that comes from unauthentic actions. In Psalm 33:13, God tells us that "From heaven the LORD looks down and sees everyone." Since God is who matters most in our lives, authenticity begins with our relationship with Him. He cannot be fooled and knows our secrets.

Jesus, as the model of authenticity, fought against the unauthentic church of His day, which was when He expressed the most anger. When He was with those who had bad reputations, *but* were authentic at other times, He felt that they were real enough to hear His words. Revelation 3:15-16 states, "I know what you are doing. I know you aren't cold or hot. I wish you were either one or the other! But you are lukewarm. You aren't hot or cold. So I am going to spit you out of my mouth." God tells us here that He'd rather have us be truthful about our present state of spirituality, even if it is to view Him negatively, than to pretend to love Him and be unauthentic. To be authentic means to turn our sin and secrets over to an authentic God for His forgiveness and empowerment. This will help us become hot water for God and not submit to the cold water forces of our culture that would demean and destroy us. Honestly facing our sin and imperfections allows us to be the authentic men God has called us to be.

Manhood Discussion - Chapter 10

1. What is your definition of an authentic man? How hard is it for you to be like your definition of an authentic man? In which areas are you most likely to pretend and not be truthful? Identify a situation where you were not authentic.

2. Identify a situation when someone was not authentic with you. How did you feel about it? What were the consequences of their lack of truthfulness with you? As father and son, identify a time when you were not authentic with each other.

3. Discuss the *Bible* verse, Matthew 10:34: "Do not think that I came to bring peace to the earth. I didn't come to bring peace. I came to bring a sword." How hard is it for you to stand up against the bad influences you encounter? In which areas of life or to whom do you have to say "No" in order to remain authentic?

4. Discuss the *Bible* verses, Revelation 3:15-16: "I know what you are doing. I know you aren't cold or hot. I wish you were either one or the other! But you are lukewarm. You aren't hot or cold. So I am going to spit you out of my mouth." What was Jesus' view of the importance of authenticity in terms of your relationship with Him?

A Lesson From The Wisdom Muffin: Make Me Proud, Become A Farmer

I was 14 and a freshman in high school. Up to this point, I never had a job and wasn't planning on having one any time soon. None of my friends were working yet, so I assumed that I would spend another summer hanging out at the local pool, enjoying late nights with my buddies, sleeping in until well past noon, only to do it all over again the next day. However, my father had a different plan for me. One day, before summer really got underway, he sat me down for one of our usual father-son discussions. Growing up in a town filled with farmland, there were quite a few farm kids in my school. These kids were always up at 5 AM, milking the cows before school and spending hours helping their fathers tend the fields after class. Their summers consisted of working long hours from dawn till dusk, learning what it is like to work for a living. My father told me that these kids were not just making money; they were learning an extremely valuable life lesson – responsibility. We are in a society where no one takes responsibility for what they do. Kids are given the easy way out. Our nation is making it easier by the day for kids to slack off and get away with loafing, as much as they want, because we have come to believe that if you force a kid to take some action and become responsible, you might damage their delicate psyche, screwing them up for life. It is rare to find a teenager who is striving to take on more responsibility; my father wanted to make sure I was one of those few kids who appreciated and understood the importance of commitment. I picked up a part-time landscaping gig and started understanding what it meant to be responsible.

I had to show up to work every day, do my job the way I was asked, admit my mistakes, and communicate with my boss on a daily basis.

Eight years later, I was out there during certain times of the summer, working 9, 10, 12 hours a day to keep on top of the landscaping. I had grown to love the responsibility I had. I took pride in my work and loved hearing how nice a yard looked when I was finished. I had proven myself reliable enough to pick my own hours and go off to job sites with no supervision. With no one looking over my shoulder, I could have easily slacked off and not taken my job seriously. Responsibility, however, would not allow me this easy and less manly option. At some point, I don't know exactly when, I began working for me and my own healthy pride, not for the one who pays me. I moved from being an employee, doing what I was told, to an owner who thinks and acts in a way that is good, no matter what the task or mission. I became a man by becoming responsible without anyone forcing me to.

Most days, I was up at 6 AM ready to start the day, only to get home around 7:00 or 8:00 at night. I did this because I accepted responsibility for my own results. I grew to cherish my work and found a reason over and above my paycheck to show up every day. One of my biggest fears was to disappoint a client because I did not take charge of my work schedule and skimped out on my work load. That driving force causes me to show up to work every day with drive and enthusiasm. Becoming responsible for a job is a way to learn how to become responsible for yourself. As men, our ability to choose well and take ownership of our choices is a key ingredient in the manhood we want to possess.

So gentlemen, in a society where accountability is considered to be of little importance, I encourage you to take a stand and start taking on your share of responsibility. Do what you can to keep yourself accountable for your actions and I promise, before you know it, you will start to develop an overwhelming feeling of pride and joy in who you are. With this pride spawns an urge for even greater responsibility; your confidence will grow as your manhood grows. Before you know it, you will have a giant circle of responsibility that produces a sense of competence, develops your skills, and helps you, as a man, make a difference in someone's life.

Manhood takes a great deal of work and anything worthwhile in life is the same. I encourage the fathers and sons who are reading this book together to read each lesson in its entirety before beginning the discussion of the chapter. I suggest that you check my words with the *Bible* to see if you agree with my thoughts. Write down your thoughts before your discussion with each other, so that you are organized and ready to share. 1 Timothy 4:8 states, "Training the body has some value. But being godly has value in every way. It promises help for the life you are now living and the life to come." Use this book as a tool, along with your *Bible* and prayer, to push one another toward becoming more godly in your walk through life together.

This journey toward manhood will be a difficult one, one that demands that you exercise and build your character. Mental sweat is expected as you ask yourself tough questions and look to each other in your relationship as father and son, to challenge each other in your growth processes. You will demonstrate respect for one another and for the time you spend together when both of you are prepared. Like any exercise program, the more you put into it, the more you'll get out of it. Manhood is *not* a right. It is something you have been called by God to accomplish, and it will take tremendous effort for you to achieve it. No one is perfect (Romans 3:10), but what God expects is that you will try, and when you do, you must try your best. The tension that was created between Jesus and the religious leaders of His day was due to their lack of even attempting to answer His difficult questions. Unlike the Pharisees, Jesus wants us to honestly communicate with Him, even if we answer His questions wrong. Together, fathers and sons are on a journey to accomplish manhood. This means that effort is necessary from both of you. In an age where we are given pretty much anything and everything we want at a moment's notice, manhood is sort of pushed to the side as it is not a gift nor is it easy to accomplish. For you to become a man, you must want it, work for it, and ask for help to attain it. Not every man is a farmer, but every man can certainly work like one.

Manhood Discussion - Chapter 11

1. Identify five responsibilities that are part of your daily life. How do you feel about the demands that life places on you? What makes the fulfillment of each of your responsibilities difficult?

2. How do you feel about the price of freedom or that of becoming a man necessitating an increase in responsibilities? When you mature, it means that you accept responsibilities that no one has given you. For the good of others and yourself, you do fulfill your responsibilities.

3. Share a dream that you have regarding your future. What work must take place for your dream to have any possibility of occurring?

4. Discuss the concept of pride and the difference between good and bad pride. How can you develop more good pride?

5. How does this *Bible* verse, "But a man who works hard values what he has" (Proverbs 12:27) relate to the topic of this chapter?

Boredom: A Man's Worst Enemy

12

As an only child, I grew bored fairly regularly. I would always ask my dad what I could do, hoping he would suggest some fun activity for me that would immediately get rid of my boredom. However, every time I asked, my father had the same answer: your boredom is your own responsibility. I understand that my father was teaching me how to take action and deal with my boredom myself. Instead of relying on him to decrease my own boredom, he wanted me to actively seek out activities that interested me and solve my own problems. As kids, we all get bored from time to time. We get restless and then get into trouble with our parents or other authorities by doing things we know we shouldn't be doing. Boredom is normal for kids, yet because of immaturity, they don't understand the boundless dangers that contribute to who they can become. When it comes to our spiritual and emotional well-being, boredom can actually encourage us to develop an important sense of curiosity and wonder about the world around us. However, when boredom sticks around throughout our childhood years and into our adolescent and adult years, it becomes quite an issue.

Before I go any further, I must clarify how I define boredom. I am sure some of you are saying that boredom cannot possibly be that big of an issue. In fact, some of the greatest inventions ever made came about because men were getting bored with their everyday, typical lifestyles and wanted to improve them. To that I say, these men were not bored, but rather, they were unsettled. A man who is unsettled knows that God is nudging him to get up off the couch and get to work. A characteristic of every great man is that he is continually never completely settled, and he knows that God is continually pushing him forward. That slight twinge, that fire in the pit of your stomach, is God telling you to continue your quest toward your edge and toward finding something else that you can master. Boredom is not a push from God, and is certainly not something a man should experience.

Now that we understand the difference between being bored and being unsettled, we can continue our discussion on why boredom is something a man should avoid. As we all know, boredom can strike at a moment's notice. When it does, we should actively seek something to do. It is at some point in the transition from our innocent years, as boys, to our not-so-innocent years, as growing men, that our boredom can really cause problems. As kids, when we are bored, we find ourselves in our backyard, digging a hole, filling it with water, and diving headfirst into this man-made pool. It seems like an excellent boredom-breaking adventure. It's relatively safe and other than ruining our dads' excellent mowing lines, it causes no real damage. However, as we get older, this sort of activity becomes boring and only increases our sense of emptiness. So instead, we turn to things that increase the level of stimulation, no matter how dangerous they may be: drugs, alcohol, sex, and other problematic activities that lead us to the slippery slope of maleness. These new and exciting adventures might seem to be a cure for our boredom, but they are dangerous. Beyond our short-term vision, we can start to see that the consequences of boredom can be rather severe.

I have shared a number of stories about my high school soccer days; all of them have relatively happy endings. However, this story is a little different. I, not quite a man and not perfect (or anywhere close to it), fell victim to boredom during my senior year of high school. Right before playoffs started, our school had our Homecoming dance, and similar to years past, kids threw parties afterwards. I didn't drink in high school. I was quite busy with feeling unsettled, striving to practice harder in sports and studying longer for tests. However, as a senior, I was bored with my studies and overconfident in myself. I decided that just this once, it was okay to drink. So, after 18 years of not touching alcohol, 15 years devoted to the game of soccer, and countless nights lying awake imagining the joys of reaching the playoffs, I had my first drink of alcohol, confessed to it, and was suspended from the team for two weeks. I apologized to those I hurt and admitted my mistakes. I did what a man would do and took full responsibility for my actions. Those around me quickly forgave me, as they saw I truly was sorry for what I had done and understood that I held myself to a higher standard and knew better. They knew I would not let this happen again. However, even with my family, friends, and teammates behind me, forgiving me, and giving me all the support in the world, I still had to sit in the stands for the next two weeks. The day before I was allowed back on the team, our team lost in our District Playoff game and our season was over. That's right, after 15 years of practicing, dreaming, wishing, hoping, praying, and working my butt off to play in a high stakes playoff game for my team, I was stuck watching the clock tick down to zero as my team lost its final match of the season. The game was close and I'm told that had I been on the pitch, I would have made a difference. It's hard to live with that guilt because I let my team down with the wrong choices that I made.

I had reoccurring nightmares for years to come about that mistake. Yes, it drove me to greater achievements in track, as I promised myself that I would not mess up like that again and that I would make it to a State Meet, no matter what. However, I can never get that final game back. Now I understand that this mistake helped keep me out of trouble and made those who are younger than me more aware that even one beer, one time, can land you in a miserable position. The underlying issue still remains: boredom caused me to have a lapse in judgment, I chose to drink and got into trouble. My boredom caused me to miss out on something I dreamed about for years and for that reason, I refuse to allow myself to become bored again.

When some of the people I mowed for happen to catch me on a break, they often expressed how impressed they were with how hard I worked, with few complaints. They would ask how I could suck it up in the hot weather on a daily basis, knowing that I was doing yard work while they enjoyed the comfort of their air-conditioned offices. My answer, then and now, is simple, yet something I hold very close to my heart: I love being busy, and it keeps me out of trouble. I understand that if I work hard and enjoy the work I do, I simply will not have time for boredom. Boredom is something that I have decided not to choose. I have learned that there is a richness that God created within me that is there to sustain me in every situation. As a man, I have a wide variety of thoughts and feelings to process. I have a God who is always there for me to talk to. How can I get bored?

Boredom happens to a young man only when he allows it. Somewhere, sometime, we are trained by life to buy into a simplistic definition of ourselves. Some of us tune out the deeper potential within us by using drugs and participating in negative behaviors that drown out our potential. We tune out a part of what God created us to be because we are not willing to do the internal work that is necessary to discover our personal richness. An odd thought, but a true one, is that God made each man with his own artistic side. The nature of each man's art is individualized, and there is diversity in its expression. For some, their art is the use of their body in athletics. Others are able to think things through and create something out of nothing. Whatever it is, the only reason we are bored is because we have failed to get in touch with the deeper, artistic parts of ourselves.

God made you in His image and with that comes a set of gifts specific to you. Boredom occurs when we fail to recognize and develop what God has given us. Our brains will be filled with dreams and ideas regarding how to expand our own giftedness if we give ourselves permission. Unfortunately, many have thrown God's gift away. They spend all of their time wanting something they do not have or trying to become something they are not. They have not put the right effort into developing their unique God-given potential with an "attitude of gratitude."

For a young male to become a man, he must look inside himself and determine which parts of himself need to be developed beyond the world that he can see. Your thoughts and feelings surround your artistic gifts, whatever they may be. When you give yourself permission to look at who you are inside, it is impossible to be bored. You must have the courage to look at what is stopping you from going forward in your area of expertise (giftedness). Maybe you have unresolved feelings about a loss that you have experienced which causes you to give up. Maybe you do not have support and encouragement from others because the people in your life do not value who you are. Maybe you are caught in some behavior that drags you down or distracts you. Your God-given energy must be placed not only on the good in life, but also on what is best for you. If you do this, there is not enough time to be bored.

Psalm 37:4 tells us, "Find your delight in the LORD. Then he will give you everything your heart really wants." This is your art, and any cheap substitute will not satisfy you. When young men get involved in activities that don't expand their giftedness, they will feel incredibly empty and unsatisfied. When they work to fulfill God's image that is within them, it excites and energizes them. The best antidote for boredom is to give yourself time to reflect on what God's gifts are for you and go full bore toward developing them.

As I understand what my giftedness is, I am able to make better choices because I know what truly matters in my life. Then, as I surround myself with a job that I am passionate about, a solid group of friends, an excellent number 1, and a burning desire to grow close to God, I can begin building a sturdy wall between boredom and myself. When temptation comes, I will be so engulfed with these more important matters that I will have less time to succumb to my wandering eye, my self-destructive tendencies, and that dark whisper from my sin nature inside telling me it will be okay, just this once.

Manhood Discussion - Chapter 12

1. How often are you bored with life? How do you feel about the concept that you have such a richness in who you are that you should never be bored? Do you accept responsibility, as a man, to take care of your own boredom when there is no one there to entertain you?

2. Share a time that you messed up. How hard was it to forgive yourself? Did you ask God for forgiveness? Did you accept the forgiveness and grace that God offers you?

3. How much time do you spend wanting something you cannot have? Share something that each of you would like to have on a material level, relational level, skill level, and spiritual level.

4. Which area(s) of your life do you see as areas of giftedness? What do you think of the term "artist," to describe this part of yourself? How can you develop this part of your life further?

5. As a man, describe seven of your top priorities. Matthew 6:33 states, "But put God's kingdom first. Do what he wants you to do. Then all of those things will also be given to you." What do you think about this *Bible* verse and how it is applied to your manhood?

Dehydration, Red Gatorade, And Gratitude

13

As men, we are quick to look to others for recognition of our contributions and value, whether that recognition is an award, a pat on the back, or a raise. When we work hard and put tremendous effort into something, we become rightfully appreciative of our accomplishments. We should want to be competent, work hard to achieve it, and feel good about God using us to help this hurting world. But what about everything that goes on behind the scenes? Men do not soar to great heights on their own. They have coaches, teachers, parents, and Bulls to help them every step of the way. Each man is given a tremendous blessing from God in the form of his talents. Yes, we work hard and put in many hours perfecting our specific talents, but we must also understand that our support system is working just as hard. These men and women are there to guide us along the way, to offer advice and help us when we fail.

A key attribute of a man is his ability to be gracious and express his gratitude. A true man understands that there are others who must be thanked for their selfless support. A man who walks this earth feeling that he owes no one a "thank you" is not a man at all. First and foremost, we must all understand that we could never reach any of our goals without The Lord. In my days of high school sports, God gave me the gift of being a good athlete. Throughout my studies in undergraduate school, He blessed me with determination and a burning desire to learn. My athletic and academic awards and achievements would not have been possible without His help. Along with His direct blessing, He also blessed me with people who were willing to help out at a moment's notice, asking nothing in return.

When I was in high school, athletes were allowed access to Gatorade in the athletic director's office on game days. We were allowed to go in at lunchtime and fill a bottle in order to start hydrating before a game. The Gatorade was always watered down, a red flavor that I never really liked. I didn't think much of it and would only take a cup at lunch, as I did it more to stay hydrated than to enjoy its taste. I took this gift for granted and often brushed it off, rather than appreciating the kindness of our athletic department. However, come game time, my attitude completely changed. Busting my hump sometimes for two 45-minute halves, up and down the field, sweating buckets, never really stopping or slowing down, I was completely drained after each game. After our games, the same red Gatorade coolers from the athletic room were placed in the locker room for us to drink, in order to get back some of the vitamins and nutrients that we lost during the game. It was the same cooler, same watered-down, gross-tasting, red Gatorade from earlier that day. However, after a brutal 90-minute game, it tasted like it was the absolute best thing I ever had the privilege of consuming in my entire life! I would chug it like it was the last thing I would ever ingest. My teammates and I would fight over the bottles, hoping we could get just one more gulp before it was gone.

How is it that the same exact drink tasted completely different after a game than it did when I wasn't completely dehydrated and dying for liquid? It was only when I was completely drained after a hard fought game that I truly appreciated the Gatorade and not only did I enjoy it, I couldn't get enough of it. As a young buck hoping to become a man, I must stress the importance of being grateful. Instead of looking at God and those around you like the watered-down, gross Gatorade served at lunch, we must see their hard work, love, and commitment to us as Gatorade after a game. We must not only appreciate them and their guidance, but actively want it, fight for it, and treat it like it could be the last gulp we'll ever have.

Sometimes, what we need to be thankful for can be packaged in a strange way, such as when being given feedback. Feedback can hurt, and yet it is necessary for keeping us hydrated. It should be one of the things in life that we automatically respond to graciously. Feedback redirects us in ways that are better than where we would be headed without it. If we seek the gift of feedback, we will be able to improve ourselves beyond what we could without it.

Males often ignore the consequences of their actions, as there is a belief that their own specialness is a protection against anything bad happening to them. The more immature we are, the more willing we are to gamble with the notion that there will be consequences for our actions. God always forgives us when He is asked, but He doesn't always remove the consequences. Part of being a man is accepting, or recognizing with gratitude, the consequences that have occurred as a result of our own actions. The acceptance that, by our actions, we get what we ask for will help us suck it up, pay restitution when necessary and learn not to choose that path again.

Another odd experience involving gratitude, as it relates to manhood, is discipline. Discipline is two-fold. First, there is self-discipline, which helps a man delay gratification and stop impulsive behavior by saying "No" to himself. Whether it is the desire to stay up longer than we should, eat something that is not good for us, or cheat on a test, we often don't want to deny our impulses; at the same time, we also understand that we are better off if we do. Studying, instead of watching TV, reaps rewards that outweigh temporary pleasure. It is likely that those who have better lives than we do, who are more successful, have learned the lost art of telling themselves "No." We need to learn to feel good when we deny ourselves a pleasure in exchange for a more long-term reward.

The second type of discipline is that of accepting correction from our parents, teachers, coaches, and other authority figures. We should consider their intervention in our lives from a manly perspective of gratitude. It means that they care about us and have a higher expectation of us than we do of ourselves. They are not going to be willing to sit idly by as we demean ourselves or put ourselves at risk. These actions on their part lets us know that they are not dependent on our affirmation in order to do what is right.

Being grateful means that who we are and what we have is enough. The more we put value in things outside of ourselves, the less satisfied we become with our lives. That's why choosing to feel good only when you have gotten a possession of some sort is a dead end street. Dealing with our insecurities by seeking a higher status often causes us to think we *need* something that, in reality, we only *want*. Learning to experience and express gratitude helps us to balance our desire to receive with our need to give. Service to others helps us to see that what we have to give has value, and to place less value on the things in life that are not as significant.

James 1:2 speaks of a paradoxical time when we should feel gratitude. It states, "My brothers and sisters, you will face all kinds of trouble. When you do, think of it as pure joy." Being tough is something that a man should want, and achieving this toughened-up state is done through some form of hardship. Just like pushing yourself in the gym produces a change in muscle structure, the trials of life lead to a change in character structure. Resiliency, or the ability to bounce back from life's kick in the butt, doesn't come without its challenges. Learning to be appreciative of this strengthening process helps you to put what you are dealing with in perspective.

1 Thessalonians 5:18 states, "Give thanks no matter what happens. God wants you to thank him because you believe in Christ Jesus." Only a man can do this regularly. God wants us to express gratitude for both the negative and positive experiences in our lives. Having the courage to own the hardships that we are experiencing, while still being thankful for God's presence, allows a person to move past what is occurring at a specific moment in time. Many males allow themselves to get stuck by obsessing on the bad times in their lives and use it to destroy themselves. Saint Paul learned to thank God and be content, no matter what state he was in, which included the times he was in jail because of his faith (Philippians 4:12). It should not matter if the Gatorade of life is the right color, your favorite flavor, or watered down; express gratitude often in a way that only a man can!

Manhood Discussion - Chapter 13

1. Make a list of ten things you are grateful for. Share your list with each other. Do not talk about being grateful for each other.

2. Share three things that you are appreciative of or grateful for in the other person.

3. How good are you at receiving feedback? Share several times when someone gave you feedback and it was helpful. How did you deal with these situations?

4. Identify a time when you had to face some negative consequences regarding a choice that you made. What did you learn from this situation?

5. 1 Thessalonians 5:18 states, "Give thanks no matter what happens. God wants you to thank him because you believe in Christ Jesus." Discuss this *Bible* verse and apply it to your discussion of this chapter. Share three things that each of you are thankful to God for.

A Lesson From The Wisdom Muffin: Some Ping Pong, Simon & Garfunkel, And Just a Hint Of Competitive Spirit

Alright, dads, this one is for you. As I've shared numerous lessons from my father that are more or less geared towards sons, I want to take a minute and give you a piece of advice I learned from my father that can be useful to you and will influence your sons and their futures in significant ways. If I haven't made it incredibly clear, my father is my most important role model, and he is the man I look up to the most in my life. I want to share a quick story with all of you fathers out there that is one of the fondest memories I have in hope of making a point about the amount of influence you have on your sons.

During my adolescent years, I had an early bedtime to ensure I was getting an adequate amount of sleep as a growing boy who was involved in a lot of afterschool programs. However, my pop also understood the importance of building a solid father-son relationship. My parents bought a ping-pong table for my birthday one year, and every night after dinner and homework, we would take turns challenging each other to a game of ping-pong. After years of playing, we became increasingly solid ping-pong players *(you are currently reading a book by the Eastern Lebanon County High School two-years-running gym class ping-pong champion, thank you very much)*. But more important than teaching me how to wield a ping-pong paddle with more accuracy and force than a deadly weapon, my father taught me something much more valuable: the importance of father-son bonding time. He would let me stay up a bit past lights out each night if it meant playing just one more game with him *(smack talk always encouraged)*. His old record player was tucked in the corner with a Simon & Garfunkel record stuck on repeat as we would sing along between bouts of panting and gasping for breath *(yes, we got that into it)*.

I still look back on the ping-pong matches with my old man and laugh about all the good times we shared, who won more matches, and what the outcome would be if we had a rematch today. To the fathers who are reading this, I want you to understand that it is the simple things like a ping-pong match a few minutes after Mom says it's time for bed, a goofy song on a beat-up record player, and a challenge from Dad saying he is certain you won't beat him if you both played left-handed that mean the most to your sons. A son does not need you to do much to impress him. He is inherently wired to love and respect you. Everything you do is being watched and taken in by your son, as he secretly tells himself that he will be just like you one day. So, take some time out of your busy schedule and do something just for fun with your son – I promise you he will never forget these seemingly pointless activities; taking your time to do them with him will be very meaningful. It is never too late to begin a relationship that includes time to simply enjoy each other's presence. A boy who has a strong father in his life is already ahead of many of his counterparts. When he fails, and he will, he won't be afraid to let you know. As he trusts and loves you, he will start to listen to you more. He will take in your wisdom and follow your instructions, which will keep him a step ahead of the other boys his age.

Every great father wants to provide for his kid and invest his time, effort, and financial support in helping him grow up and become a successful man. Just remember that, sometimes, all it takes is a few minutes, some funky music, and a ping-pong table to make a world of difference to your kid. Find something he enjoys and learn to love it as well. As a father, you have a burning desire to provide for your son; you want to work hard to provide a safe life and a bright future for him. However, as fathers, you can sometimes become overly focused on providing for your son and start to neglect spending time with him. Take some time out from providing *for* him and start spending time *with* him.

As you work on this manhood journey together, part of what is expected is that you spend at least *some* time together. If I was to decide on the ideal amount of fun time for you to spend together, I would suggest at the *minimum*, one to two hours per week. In a life filled with agendas, I encourage you to fill this time slot with the agenda of *NO AGENDA*. This is time to enjoy one another, whether it is a ping-pong match like my father and I had, a fishing trip, or a hike. The responsibility for planning this time should be rotated between you and your son as you each share the things in life you both enjoy. Whatever you decide to do during this "nothing" time, I must emphasize the importance of being committed to this guaranteed time together. There should be very few things in life that would cause this father-son time to be cancelled. This time of laughter and sharing interests prepares you for the more challenging parts of this program. If I went to my father for guidance or support, I am certain that, out of the 31,536,000 seconds in a year, there is not a single second that he would consider more important.

The same is true for our relationship with God. Too often we are willing to skimp out on our time with God because we are not comfortable with Him. We live our lives in our own little world and ignore His messages (through nature, relationships with others, the *Bible*, to name a few). When we trip up in life, we rush to Him with our weakened faith and expect Him to handle the more difficult decisions for us. It would increase our trust in God if we would give ourselves more time to become familiar with Him. Jesus serves as an excellent example of how to invest our time. He prioritized its use so that He took care of His significant relationships and had enough time to refuel Himself. How we fuel ourselves is an important task that we should complete in conscious ways. Jesus demonstrated how to keep up His energy by regularly having conversations with His Father. He set boundaries with people who depleted Him. He spent increased amounts of time with those who were supportive of Him and emotionally close to Him. He knew well (and often quoted) the Old Testament.

We each have an internal computer that flashes red warning lights when we are about to break. Maybe it is in the form of anger, tearfulness, shutting down, or a strong desire to behave in a certain negative way. Manhood means accepting our limits when we are exhausted and recognizing when we need to reboot. When this red light begins to flash, it is our internal warning system telling us we are doing a bit too much and need to take a step back and spend some time relaxing; if we don't, we will soon become overwhelmed *(if you need a visual example of people who are overwhelmed, simply take a trip to a college campus during finals week)*. Knowing when we need to reboot and how to reboot our internal computer properly are important manhood tasks. My dad is a great ally when it comes to a proper reboot; our time together always strengthens me for the challenging days ahead. When that red light begins to flash, a good left-handed ping-pong game will immediately turn it off. What, or *who*, fuels you?

Manhood Discussion - Chapter 14

1. Share with your son what it was like the day he was born or the day you brought him home. Discuss two memories that you each have of times that you enjoyed being together. Dad – share a memory from your childhood, good or bad, that your son doesn't know about.

2. What are the things you each do individually for fun that refuel you? Discuss a list of activities that you can do together for two hours of refueling time, as mentioned in this chapter. Identify a time that would be good for both of you to do this?

3. What is your favorite type of music? Pick a song that you like and listen to it together. Share why you like it.

4. Dad, talk to your son about three areas of life that you think he should know about. Share your words of wisdom or the thoughts you have that are related to each of these areas.

5. Luke 6:12-13 states, "On one of those days, Jesus went out to a mountainside to pray. He spent the night praying to God. When morning came, he called for his disciples to come to him. He chose 12 of them and made them apostles [followers]." Apply these *Bible* verses to your discussion of this chapter. What did Jesus do to refuel? How did his refueling time relate to the decision He had to make?

The Top Five Decisions That Determine A Man's Future (Part 1)

15

How can I limit a young boy's future to only five life-determining decisions? It takes hundreds of intricate, well-coordinated pieces working together to keep this machine of a boy perfectly tuned to make him ready to grow toward becoming a man. I do admit, there are thousands of issues, topics, scenarios, and life lessons that have gone into developing me into a young man. If I were to narrow it down to the top five, I can rattle them off without thinking twice. To those fathers who are reading this book, I want to stress that there is a difference between an older man reading this book and a boy in his early teens to early twenties reading it. If you were to ask me what it takes to turn an adult male into a man and limit this transition to five decisions which are key, I wouldn't have the slightest clue. But, the question I am asking is how do we mold a young boy into a strong, determined man with a bright future? The following approach can help our youth.

I am going to lay out all five decisions together, then go into detail on each one in the following paragraphs. There is no one decision that takes priority over the others, so you can choose to read them in any order you want. I will number them to make it easy for you to know where one ends and another starts. I repeat, the order you read them in makes no difference, as long as you read them, gents! The five decisions are: pick a profession that suits you, surround yourself with Bull Elephants, choose your *close* friends wisely, devote yourself to God (those of you who have not identified with a belief system, devote yourself to a power that is greater than you), and lastly, learn the difference between failure and quitting.

1. Pick a profession that suits you. I understand that some of you who are reading this book are a bit young to be thinking about what you want to be working on for the rest of your lives, but it is never too early to start asking yourself what your passion is and what you are great at. A man who loves his job will not work a day in his life. There have been very few days that my father actually "worked." He realized very early in his life that he had a great passion for helping others and counseling them through hard times. When he sets foot into his office, he is not working for a paycheck, but expressing his God-given giftedness. He goes to work because he loves what he does. When a man works simply for money, he finds himself caught in a trap that is impossible to get out of. This trap occurs when a person decides that satisfaction is a result of material things when, in reality, satisfaction only comes from living a life that fulfills our essence, as God created us to be.

A man who can find peace and happiness at work is a man who will learn to enjoy every other aspect of his life. He doesn't allow others to define his importance by the status they give him based on his job. He is able to shed his work clothes (literally and figuratively) when he comes home, along with the troubles from his day. He is not defined by his job; he defines his job. He learns to cherish his time with his family and devote his full attention and love to them when he is at home. When a man works with passion and enjoys what he does, his attitude positively influences others. He works harder and smarter, and does not let bumps in the road slow him down. When faced with a problem, he resolves it by hunkering down and seeing it as a challenge that he can meet, rather than running from it.

Finding the right profession helps a man enjoy what he does every day rather than daydreaming of what could have been. You need to discover what your gifts are and find ways to express them. You must learn to appreciate the opportunities you have to express your giftedness more than the financial rewards that you receive as a result of your gifts. Satisfaction always beats having possessions. Although working on our weaknesses is helpful, most of our energy should be spent developing the gifts that God has given us and then, using them to help others.

2. Surround yourself with Bull Elephants. I have been blessed to have a life which is filled with Bull Elephants. These men taught me valuable life lessons and guided me through some very difficult times and transitions. By surrounding yourself with Bull Elephants you are lining up in battle next to some of the toughest, most hard-nosed, combative soldiers on the planet. These men have been to hell and back, all the while learning countless life lessons. They do not impart knowledge just to hear themselves talking. They have traveled the path before you, screwed up majorly, and are sharing their wisdom with you in hopes that you will achieve and become more than they have so far. These are our nation's true leaders. They do not cling to the past or live vicariously through their protégés; instead they are overwhelmed with pride and joy when you accomplish the great feats that they themselves have not. These Bulls will be hard on you and will hold you accountable. They are honest men who live with a purpose. They will not allow you to take advantage of them or of others, and more importantly, they will not allow you to demean yourself. They will be hard, but they will be fair. They understand the difficult, demanding path that you are on and will be there when you stumble. Most importantly, these men will not protect you from failure. They will allow you to fail, but not to quit. Through failure comes growth and knowledge. These Bulls understand that the many, many times they failed, lessons were learned which contributed to their growth.

1 John 1:9 explains, "But God is faithful and fair. If we admit that we have sinned, he will forgive us our sins. He will forgive every wrong thing we have done. He will make us pure." As the ultimate goal in our lives, God has prepared, through the death of His Son, for us to be forgiven when we fail. At times, this demands that we examine our lives for what is taking us backward and confess these issues to God. As promised, God forgives us and looks for our desire to change. Jesus lived perfectly and died in our place for our imperfections. As a result, we no longer have to quit, for God has prepared a way for us to be restored so that we can once again become young men of His calling.

Manhood Discussion - Chapter 15

1. List the top five decisions that you would like to write about. As you look back on your life, share a good decision that you made, or reflect upon a bad decision that you made and then share what you should have done differently.

2. Share the type of job that you think fits your skills. Dad, state several things that you either like or don't like about your job. Son, talk about what you like and don't like about your job. If you do not have a job yet, share what kind of job you think you would like as a teenager and the type of job that you would like to do as an adult.

3. Identify three Bull Elephants and two women who have taught you something valuable. What did you learn from them?

4. Identify a failure that you experienced within the last two weeks. What did you learn from this failure that will assist you in not repeating it?

5. 1 John 1:9 states, "But God is faithful and fair. If we admit that we have sinned, he will forgive us our sins. He will forgive every wrong thing we have done. He will make us pure." Apply this *Bible* verse to your discussion of this chapter.

The Top Five Decisions That Determine A Man's Future (Part 2)

16

3. Choose your *close* friends wisely. You can't always pick who you have to deal with in life. More times than not there is some moron in the room with you who you may fantasize about sucker-punching square in the jaw. But, besides the typical jerks that we find around every corner, there are diamonds in the rough. These are the guys we know who will always have our back. These are the guys you can hang out with for hours on end and not have to say *a single word*. You feel so comfortable with them, that you can simply just do nothing when you are with them. Conversation is never forced; arguments are quickly forgiven and forgotten. But, more important than just being a good time and that group of guys who "gets you," these blokes are the guys who are constantly hounding you and are up your backside about staying on course. When you wander off into the shadows of lies and deceit, they quickly yank you back and pummel you into the dirt to make certain you never mess up like that again.

When you have a solid group of friends who are unwavering in their belief structure and outlook on life, they are like the Russian Secret Police – they are constantly watching you. Even when you are totally alone, you know they are watching. Now, I don't mean literally watching you, with secret spy cameras and hidden microphones. What I mean is, once you establish this core group of friends, each one having a solid foundation, you begin to hold yourself to their standards. When you are not around them and are tempted to stray from the right path, you are more likely to fight the urge to regress due to the higher sense of accountability that you have with these friends. It is one thing to lie to yourself and convince yourself that it is okay to wander from the path every once in a while. But, to lie to your closest allies is an entirely different story. The image you have of their support is with you even when you're alone.

Every man has a burning desire to have a close friend to rely on and to trust. With this desire also comes a desire to be an equal in that relationship and to give to this friend as he gives to you. No man wants to upset the people who trust him; he understands that if he screws up they will find out and the relationship will be scarred by his deceit, thus weakening the bond between them. Now, this is not to say that if you do screw up, your friends should immediately abandon you, because we all screw up and the people who love us the most are the ones who are there for us first. They let you know the pain that you've caused and their willingness to help you grow after your mistakes, rather than simply forgetting about them.

Proverbs 27:17 states, "As iron sharpens iron, so one person sharpens another." You and I have the uncanny ability to fool ourselves by believing our own lies. There are many ways we can get in trouble by overestimating our capabilities and underestimating our ability to mess up. It is our friends who care enough about us to confront us and keep us safe. We are safer hearing things we don't want to hear from others, and dealing with them, than pretending that the rules of life do not apply to us. I have been blessed with many close friends. One of the attributes that is a personal requirement for me to define someone as a close friend is his ability to tell me the truth and confront me. It is through disagreement with my friends that I have gained a greater appreciation for their strengths and their willingness to be real men in my life. I have benefited from a number of guys who don't put up with my crap and tell me like it is. Often, these men are God's representatives in my life; they tell me when to slow down, and when to stop my foolish behavior, try something new, and stop focusing on myself.

4. Devote yourself to God (someone greater than yourself). A male who walks this earth only to live for himself is no man in my book. In order to be a man, you must sacrifice your very soul for something much greater

than yourself. For me, that sacrifice is to God, because without Him we would obviously not have the talents He has given us. The Lord blessed me with a swift mind and a sharp tongue which helps me convey His messages to others. He has placed me in a special environment that will give me support, enough trials to develop myself, and a path that honors Him through my willingness to help others. Each of you must determine what it is that God has blessed you with and use these God-given tools to help those less fortunate than you. Not only has God blessed you with the gift of life, the tools you need to help you improve the lives of others, and the gift of internal happiness if you choose it, He has given you an amazing opportunity to fight for something greater than yourself. Through the love of Christ, many men have gone on to do tremendous works and heroic deeds. He helps men overcome their fears and leads them into battle, whispering to them that He has their back and is ready for whatever attacks them. By trusting in God, a man knows that he will always come out victorious. Yes, we will lose many battles in this boxing match we call life, but after the final round, no matter what the score is, we know we will be walking back to the locker room with our coach, Jesus Christ, as a champion.

Wear your team colors proudly and never back down from an opponent; the Lord does not care if you win every tournament. He only wants you to be a man of God who is unwavering in his faith and ready to do battle at a moment's notice. God makes a promise in Hebrews 13:5, "God has said, 'I will never leave you. I will never desert you.'" Believe it or not, He means it! Revelation 3:20 states, "'Here I am! I stand at the door and knock. If any of you hears my voice and opens the door, I will come in and eat with you. And you will eat with me.'" Jesus stands by wanting to come into your life, if you simply ask Him. Submitting your will to His will allows you to become the champion He has called you to be. The submission to a power outside of ourselves, although initially unpleasant and humbling, is the only true way to go. When left to our own devices, we end up making negative decisions which then prevent us from becoming what we ultimately could be.

5. Learn the difference between failure and quitting. A while back, my mentor, close friend and uncle, Roy Smith, made me make a promise to

him. He made me swear that I would never quit, no matter what. To this day, I have held onto that promise and have not quit on anything I have attempted. Roy taught me the difference between failure, which is something we must all go through, and quitting, which is something real men never do. To make my point clear, I want to go back to my days as a high school soccer player. Each year, our school holds a tournament at the beginning of the season in order to help us prepare for the upcoming regular season games. Our coach never invited the schools in our District; instead, he invited the soccer power-houses throughout the state of Pennsylvania. The schools that would come to our tournament would be a lot bigger and have records that were far better than ours. These schools were big, scary, mean, nasty, and downright dirty. The tournament got our attention quickly and made us aware that the season would be filled with a lot of blood, dirt, aches, and pains. The tournament that was held during my senior season proved to be the most difficult one that our team played during all four years of high school. All three teams that we played were, on average, a head taller than each of us, had about twenty pounds on each of us, and when stacked against us, made our team look like little boys in the shadow of full-grown men. Their beards were something to admire.

These teams were an intimidating sight to say the least, with resumes that included District and State Champions over numerous years. Our team managed to pull through to the final and was ready for battle against the past year's State Champions. I would like to tell you that, by not quitting when pitted against these monsters, we came out victorious and held the trophy above our heads in triumph. However, that was not the case. We lost the final match of the tournament, but it was a close game. Not once during that game did any of my teammates quit. We got pushed around, knocked down, and completely flattened for 99% of the game. But, we pressed on until the final whistle. When the game was over and our opponents were celebrating their victory, we too were celebrating, quietly. Yes, we didn't beat them, but our team was able to hang with a team that was much better than we were. That's pretty impressive, if you ask me.

You see, it would have been easy to give up and quit after the first time we were knocked off the ball. We could have thrown in the towel and let our teammates do the work while we half-assed it up and down the field, saying to ourselves, "It's over" before it started, and quit. Instead, we played our hearts out for the entire game. Did we fail? Absolutely! Did we quit? Not once. I am still so proud of what my teammates did during those 90 minutes of play, and I am certain it is because none of them quit. I am equally sure that you must stop making quitting an option. Failure is something we must all deal with, because through failure comes growth, and when we are growing, we are open to ways we can improve ourselves. Once a man quits, he is giving up a part of himself that he can never get back. Never quit, gentlemen. It's simply not worth it!

Young David was willing to fail and never quit, even in the face of the giant, Goliath. Adult men weren't able to stand up for what was right in this situation or see the power of God that they could have asked for. But, David trusted God and used his own strategy instead of fighting the way that others said he should. In battle, as warriors of God, we must be authentic and fight in ways that fit our personal giftedness. Many young men quit before they ever get a chance to fail simply by choosing not to be themselves. Posing and using another person's approach is quitting without acknowledging it. When learning from our Bulls, we must keep in mind that we must create our own paths, for God calls us to be ourselves.

Manhood Discussion - Chapter 16

1. List five characteristics of a good friend. Describe the strengths and weaknesses that you have, as a friend. What do you look for in a friend? What are the good features of your friendship with each other?

2. Identify a time that you were confronted by a friend and were helped, as a result. When have you cared enough about a friend to confront him/her? What happened? How do the two of you communicate when you disagree with each other? How can you both improve this interaction?

3. What do you think about God and the possibility of having a relationship with Him? How difficult is it for you to talk to God (through prayer) and to study His Word?

4. Are there any issues in your life that are causing you to feel like quitting? How can you keep yourself going? Share a situation in which you decided to quit, and in retrospect wished you hadn't.

5. Revelation 3:20 states, "Here I am! I stand at the door and knock. If any of you hears my voice and opens the door, I will come in and eat with you. And you will eat with me." Apply this *Bible* verse to your discussion of this chapter.

Balance, Cooperation, The Adventure, And Number 1

At first glance, this chapter may appear to be the most boring one in the book. Devoted to the subject of women and all the mushy, gushy things that go along with women, I'm certain it's a topic none of us really *want* to read. In fact, I don't even want to write about it, let alone read about it. However, as growing, maturing men, we need to cover all the bases, and the issue of women is one of utmost importance in manhood. This is the chapter that many of us don't want to read because we are tired of health class lectures on the do's and don'ts of dating. Many of you will be tempted to skip this chapter, thinking that it'll be just like everything else you've been told about dating, boundaries, and the like. You may think it will turn into some gross love story where the heroic knight rescues the beautiful princess, and they whisk off to his castle on his brilliant white steed where they are promptly married and live happily ever after. When I wrote that sentence, even *I* cringed. So, I promise, this chapter won't be anything like that. No textbook junk, no princess-rescuing, nothing like what has been putting us to sleep since preschool.

Before this book was published, many, if not most, of the older men who were proofreading the rough draft, asked me why this topic was not in *The Top Five Decisions That Determine a Man's Future*. I convinced them that the following actions must be established in a young male's heart in order for him to become a man: find his profession through the identification of his passion, devote himself to God (someone greater than himself), surround himself with Bulls, understand the difference between failure and quitting, and choose your close friends wisely. However, the idea of close friends being *more* important than finding a woman to spend the rest of one's life with was something they didn't immediately understand. You see, I believe it is more important to become a man first, before you invite a woman into the picture. At our age, we often move too quickly when it comes to women and relationships. We believe that finding a woman to date, grow close to and begin to understand will, in turn, help us understand ourselves and our value. The truth is that we need to figure ourselves out first. We must discover what we're interested in, define our values, and our purpose, and develop our strengths before we look for a woman to share our lives with. A little understood concept in psychology has proven that, as humans, we are attracted to, and attract those who have the same maturity level as we have. If we say that 1 = crazy and 10 = strong, self-determined, and wise, a man, regardless of what his own number is, will be on the lookout for a woman with a similar number. He will pick a person with a similar number, based on his own maturity level. If you are a 5, you'll date 5s; if you're a 7, you'll date 7s, and so on. Every once in a while, you might date a person with a number higher or lower than your own number, but often, that relationship will not last long. You are better off if you start dating after you have developed yourself because only then are you looking for the right things in a relationship.

So, how is it that finding a woman to settle down with was not in *The Top Five Decisions That Determine A Man's Future*? The reason is that it was my top *sixth* choice for very good reasons. I believe a young boy must get a handle on his top five decisions, at least for the most part, before he can start making decisions about finding a woman to marry. I look at it this way – How can I figure out a girl if I haven't even figured myself out yet?

A lot of people, especially young females, claim that young men do not know what *commitment* means. Yes, there are young males out there who are immature and refuse to commit to anything in life, especially a relationship with a woman. These males may look at women as something to possess, not someone to be with. The sexual aspects of a relationship are emphasized because they care about themselves and their needs rather than about who she is. It's sad, because they define her as less human by objectifying her. They limit the development of their own potential.

However, I think there is something deeper at play here. Young males in our society do not know what the word *balance* means. Look around you. Young males are giving 100% to the activities and interests they choose, which is a form of commitment. More and more young males are learning the importance of higher education, and are committing more to their studies, hoping to get accepted into a college, and even grad school. Our high school and college wrestlers devote months on end to training, and they also choose to give up sweets and carbs to cut weight for the season. Track stars are running farther and training longer; football players are getting stronger and our soccer stars are more skilled. Why? Because young men are committing themselves to these activities, and making sure that they are the best they can be. In fact, young men are committing their very lives by signing up for the Armed Forces, so it is clearly not commitment that we lack, but *balance*.

This lack of understanding regarding how to balance all parts of our lives is not, I repeat, *not* as difficult a task to master as some might believe. You can see young boys and men balance the various parts of their lives. The boys who are committed to their sport will balance practice and studying to make sure that they do not get placed on academic probation. Guys are able to balance the multiple parts of their lives, including family, church, time spent with friends, sports programs (sometimes three or four at a time), and studying. However, when it comes to balancing *life* and *girls*, something gets a little screwy.

So, how do we fix this? How can we start creating a balance between life and girls? My summer league soccer coach never said much. He would stand there in silence during every game and at every halftime, his speech would be the same, telling us to get our thumbs out of a certain body part and play like we meant it. However, there was one piece of information he gave us that really applies to the issue of finding the right girl. He would tell us that often each 90-minute game was decided by the first 30 seconds, because how we start something is usually how it ends up. This also holds true for any relationship.

The first problem young boys have is that they screw up the first few weeks or months of a new relationship by choosing girls that are likely to become dependent on them. A dependent woman is much safer to deal with because she is less likely to reject you. Many guys confuse love with dependency. However, these two attributes are miles apart. True love is based on choice; it is not forced or part of a demand. A man can be there for protection, support, and guidance, but a *true*, loving relationship is one of cooperation, not of dependency.

At the start of most relationships, both parties throw everything they have at each other. In my opinion, the way they go at this can be downright annoying. All they think, know, or care about is the other person. They are tuned in to each other at very high levels, while trying their hardest to let the other one know how much they care and truly want this newly-formed relationship to work. They shrink life down, making it just about them and them alone. Sometimes, panic and fear set in, as they try to present themselves in the "right light," rather than just being who they are, authentically. Unfortunately, no one can keep up this kind of act for long. The main point is this: start your relationship off right. The entire relationship will be decided by the first few days or weeks. Instead of throwing everything including the kitchen sink at her, take things slow, be yourself, and don't get caught up in the rush of emotions that you'll experience in the beginning of the relationship.

It is at the start of the relationship that you must let the young woman know you have multiple priorities in your life which you will need to balance with the time you spend with her. You will also need to expect that she has goals in her life and is growing in ways that don't include you. You both may play multiple sports, have more homework than ever before, attend church, do volunteer work, and have family obligations. It is during the first stages of a relationship that you need to let the girl, who is a potential number 1 in your heart, know that you have a lot of obligations in your life, and just because you are busy, it does not mean that she is not important. If you can establish this reality early in the relationship, it will sink in and she will either dump you or understand and support you. Now fellas, if she dumps you, that just shows that she wasn't truly a potential number 1. If she can't support the multiple obligations in your life, don't sweat it! Her affirmation doesn't define who you are, *you do*!

Let's return to the discussion of finding a solid group of close friends. A young male needs to surround himself with others who are firm in their beliefs and steadfast in the face of opposition, both of which we have already discussed. However, on a more basic level, close friends serve as a foundation for the rest of a young buck's life. They are an important resource for supporting a marriage for the long-term, because friendships with other adult men will meet important needs that a woman can't. Think back on all of the memories you have as a kid and a teenager. For many of us, they are not memories of being alone, wishing you had friends, but memories filled with close friends! These events in our lives help shape us into who we will be. I am certain that a young boy who establishes a close group of friends who have good standards will be much better off later in life. The interpersonal skills developed during these early friendships will create a strong foundation for making a decision on who we will marry.

Unfortunately, what often happens once a girl comes into the picture? This young male starts devoting all his time to her and starts neglecting his friends. He ignores them when they say she isn't right for him, or that he has changed and never wants to hang out with his buds anymore. He thinks that he knows what's best, has it all together, and continues soaking up the great times with his girl. He doesn't recognize the cost he is paying as he limits his connections with his other friends. He starts to change and he loses his support system, as his world narrows. In a few months, if she dumps him for the new boy in school, he finds himself alone. *If he is extremely lucky*, his friends will welcome him back into the group, without saying the obvious "I told you so." But, what about the boys who don't get dumped? They will eventually experience what happens when they neglect their support group. These boys will have no one to fall back on and more importantly, no one to be accountable to; they are much more likely to veer off the path (not just when it comes to boundaries with dating, but in all aspects of life). A guy will always treat the people he has relationships with better if he has a team of solid friends to support him. When he disconnects from his support team for a romantic relationship, he will hurt himself and the other people in his life. It is these friends that keep him in line when it comes to right and wrong, and without this core group, a young boy is likely to slip and fall, taking an innocent girl with him. His support team helps him discover the right woman, because they know him and have no agenda for his life outside of what is best for him.

Now that we understand the first two keywords when dealing with women: *balance* and *cooperation*, we can move on to the third and fourth keywords. While they are growing up, young boys are told stories of knights in shining armor rescuing damsels in distress who, for the most part, are helpless and *need* these knights to come to their rescue. The knight rescues the damsel, they fall in love, and live happily ever after. Besides the fact that these stories are stupid and pointless, they start our young boys off with stories that point them toward the wrong path. For this approach to work, we would first need to find a weak girl who we are attracted to. However, we need to be aware that if we do find this girl, we would end up shooting ourselves in the foot because we would not have a strong partner. A strong partner limits our negative desires to dominate and control. We all have a tendency to be too self-focused.

Young boys start to internalize this fantasized adventure and, sooner or later, start to make the *women* the adventure. We are taught from a young age, directly and indirectly, that girls like being the adventure. We are taught that women love to be captured by an evil villain and fought for by a fearless knight. They want to be like a trophy which the better team wins. However, this is not true. Women want to be *part* of the adventure, not *the adventure*. See the difference? Women want to go along for the ride, not be the ride. As soon as a young male makes a potential number 1 *the adventure*, the relationship is lost. We must understand that any woman who is worthy of being our number 1 is a woman who wants to go *along* for the ride and enjoy life's adventures with us, not be the adventure that must be conquered.

Lastly, and most importantly, we need to understand the importance of the term, number 1. I've been throwing the term, *number 1*, around like it's a seed in a race; I want to explain the tremendous importance that *number 1* really has. The concept of *number 1*, once understood, can encourage us to appreciate women more, and help us make more of a conscious effort to find our true number 1. Think of something in your life that you value; it can be a memory, your car, a friend, *or even a par-*

ent, and prioritize its significance with a numerical value. That number is equivalent to the potential love that your heart can give to that aspect of your life. You can't treat all relationships the same, because your time is limited. You need to rank order your priorities, no matter how much you don't want to think about it. But when it comes to your number 1, you'd need to take one of those parts of your life with its ranking, multiply it by 10, then another 10, and maybe a third and fourth 10. You can only have one number 1 relationship because the deepest level of intimacy cannot occur with more than one person. So, who you marry needs to be the only person in the number 1 slot. That slot may be empty, but another relationship can't fill the needs you have. You can have more people in your number 2 slot (like your parents and family); but only one relationship can fit in the number 1 slot. It creates a problem if one of our parents treats us like we are number 1 when we know it shouldn't be this way because they can't be *our* number 1. We can love them, but we can't meet their needs as a peer. God gave man (and woman) a burning desire to love a significant other. It has been biologically wired into us since man first walked the earth.

For most of us, God wants us to eventually have a relationship with someone who will be closer to us than we are to our parents. When we form this relationship it means that the person must be good enough to offer us love and commitment beyond what we have experienced so far within our families. We have to be grown up enough that we are no longer dependent on our parents. As they have been number 1 with each other and love us as one of their number 2s, we must be ready to emotionally accept that we are ready to find our own number 1. We should practice getting to know women by discovering the different types of personalities they have, and by learning how we relate to each type of personality. Just as we can respect the different people in our lives, but do not necessarily have them as friends, we need to find the type of woman that fits our style, just as we fit hers. Trying to form a relationship with any woman without considering our personality styles fails to recognize our differences. Dating, when done right, makes the timing of a deeper commitment through marriage and the reasons for it clearer.

The biology of the male and female genders draws us toward each other. However, our biology can act as a distraction when we are getting to know each other. No matter what you like about a woman, there will be differences. Some of these differences will be deal-breakers and the relationship will end. This causes pain, but it can be worked through and you can move past it, rather than continuing a harmful relationship. If you must end a bad relationship, do so quickly, guillotine style (*you know, whack! – and it's over*), rather than trying to "saw off" the relationship, butter knife style, which causes much more pain. This is the most humane way to break up, so that both of you can quickly begin to heal. Endless conversations about the potential for continuing a relationship drains both of you and is not worth the time. If a relationship starts off with both sides straining to make it work, if and when it leads to marriage, the marriage is almost certainly doomed to divorce, or at the very least to misery. All relationships require work. If a relationship is a lot of work early on, get out of it.

2 Corinthians 6:14 states, "Do not be joined to unbelievers. What do right and wrong have in common? Can light and darkness be friends?" This verse points out that having the same values is a primary factor in the long-term success of a relationship. If there are differences in a couple's beliefs about God, He cannot help them work through the inevitable challenges that are part of any relationship. Many marriages come to a point where divorce is the only option, short of murder. When God is a part of the couple's dialogue, He can help to limit the relationship from progressing beyond what it should be, if it is not His will. God is there to help both of you, as believers, get through the difficult process of becoming friends and discontinuing the romantic attachment. Usually during this transition, it is helpful to limit your time together, as each person needs to heal before a non-romantic friendship can form. We need to practice relating to different women, because we will actually be different with each of them. Prematurely limiting our dating to one person is not beneficial.

Unfortunately, our culture seems to say "Find a girl, and keep her." We have to be careful before we make any commitment that is for a lifetime. To find that number 1, we need God to guide us in the right direction. This most important human relationship is worth waiting for.

Manhood Discussion - Chapter 17

1. For the Son: How important is it for you to have a girlfriend or to be dating? What do you think about the concept that the stronger you are as a man, the stronger the woman will be who is attracted to you? What characteristics are you looking for in a girlfriend?

   For the Dad: Share honestly how you have done in your search for number 1. What characteristics do you feel are important for a number 1 relationship?

2. How much significance do you give the concept that a man defines his worth, not the woman with whom he has a relationship? Identify a male who has hurt himself by being involved with a female who was not good for him. How do you know when someone you are interested in is not good for you?

3. It has been said that one of the biggest competitors with true love is dependency. What does that mean? Do you agree with the statement that a young man should keep a balance between his time with his friends and his time with his girlfriend? If you are dating, how important is it to get your friends' and your family's opinion of how well you and your girlfriend fit together?

4. What characteristics do each of you have that women would appreciate in a relationship? What characteristics do each of you have that women would not appreciate? Is it easy for you to be cooperative in your relationships or are you more likely to be oppositional? Have you ever had to end a relationship with any male or female? Did you do it butter knife-style or guillotine-style?

5. 2 Corinthians 6:14 states, "Do not be joined to unbelievers. What do right and wrong have in common? Can light and darkness be friends?" What does this *Bible* verse mean in relation to the topic of this chapter?

Private: Stay Out

18

Before modern pre-birth imaging, the moment of birth was centered on one of two pronouncements: "It's a boy!" or "It's a girl!" What did everyone's eyes turn to, to make sure an immediate, no-doubt distinction could be made? The answer is that there is either something called a penis between the baby's legs or another physical formation that is less visually obvious. A baby boy, it is said, has already found his penis while in the womb, and having this body appendage is not a surprise to him. By this time, he has already been seen touching it, within the womb, and is seemingly interested by its presence. It also appears that he enjoys touching it and can actually become agitated as a result of this activity. Life progresses, and soon he is a toddler, walking and talking. He is saying names as people point to his face or theirs. You hear him identify eyes, nose, mouth, and ears, as he answers the numerous pop quizzes given to him by friends and relatives. The young boy might quietly start to wonder why one of his favorite areas of the body, his penis, is not mentioned in these quizzes. Why, when he touches it in public *(short of the latest rap video)* do the relatives all get quiet, look away, or say, "Not now!" He wonders, "What is now?" There is a strange fascination that emerges in this young boy. He has a physical part that creates sensations which are both pleasant and agitating. At times, when the world seems out of balance, he may find that touching it is calming and soothing. Yet, no one talks about this part of him.

While in the bathroom with his siblings or in other settings, he begins to understand that girls do not have this part, and looking at Dad, he goes "wow." He picks up on the social cues that his enjoyment of his penis should not be expressed publicly, and frankly, in most situations he has to pretend it doesn't exist at all. Short of playing doctor (and getting in trouble for it) with neighborhood kids, no discussion of this body part occurs. As he gets older, he may compare his penis to the penises of other boys his age, or he may be dared to touch someone else's genitals, or his may be touched. However, touch games that are a form of exploration occur in secret. Often, no one talks to him about his penis, why it feels good to touch it, and how to use it beyond peeing. If he is victimized, an older peer or adult may inappropriately introduce him to the sexual aspects of his penis and he ends up confused, traumatized, and hurt (one out of every six to ten boys are abused). This creates a life of increased secrecy, as he repeatedly asks himself, "Why me?"

Parents continue to teach the young boy a lot about life. They tell him about God and take him to church, where stories of Jesus abound. They teach him how to fill the toilet paper holder; they send him off to school, and help him learn to read, as well as many other life skills. Except for a possible emergency situation, where his penis is noticed, life goes on for a while. Emergencies could occur when parents interrupt a discovery session with his peer group, or if he meets a sexual perpetrator who wants to use him. Despite all of the training he gets regarding things he isn't curious about, education regarding his penis and its sexual function comes sporadic at best. Yes, there are parents who gracefully bring up its sexual purpose, but often the emphasis is decidedly on its reproductive functions. The best (or worst) source of information about his penis continues to be from talk on the school bus, as the older kids seem to relish sharing their knowledge of this intriguing area of life with those who are younger.

If you are reading this book, it is likely that when you are naked, if you look down you will see a penis. We are going to talk briefly about your sexuality and how it fits within your manhood. This is a very important aspect of who you are, and many of you have been trying to define it for years. There are plans to write another book called *Being God's Man.* Since this subject is both significant and complex, we will deal with it in more detail in the next book. Your father (mentor) and you have already formed your own patterns of either talking or not talking about your sexuality. You know that your penis feels good when it is touched outside of a bathroom activity. Many mornings when you wake up, it will be erect and seem ready for some type of action.

One of the goals of this brief chapter is to help you realize that sexuality is an important part of your life. It was created by God, not only for procreation, but to be used for your pleasure in a relationship with a woman you are committed to, in marriage. Although a woman looks different from you, her genital region was also created for pleasure, as well as for reproduction. When two people, who love each other and are committed to each other, express themselves in this way, their love gets stronger. Did you know that when your semen is released inside of her, there is a chemical within your semen that increases your emotional bond with her? This same chemical is found in breast milk and increases the emotional bond between a baby and its mother.

As a young man grows up, he becomes more aware of his biological nature and the pleasure function that his penis can provide. This is normal; it also creates an increased opportunity for him to grow in his manhood. To guide your sexual instincts responsibly is to take your manhood seriously. For some, it will be the biggest challenge of manhood. The culture that you live in may work to stimulate this part of your life in unhealthy ways, and fail to connect it to the meaning that God intended. Many men have returned to immaturity by failing to guide their sexual desires by using them solely for pleasure.

Unfortunately, because the pleasure-responsibility balance has been so misused in the history of man, the typical pattern of parental interaction regarding the penis, which was mentioned at the beginning of this chapter, has occurred. Many adults have adopted the unfortunate strategy of "if we don't talk about sex and your penis, you won't notice it." Well, you have! Your dad has too, and it's time for you two to talk about what it means. If you have already experienced your sexuality with your peers, let it go. It is what often happens before manhood is reached. If someone has touched you without your permission, in a way that was weird or uncomfortable, please talk to your dad about it or email us for assistance at bull@knightsofthe21stcentury.com. For any of you who are fathers, if you have had an experience that was painful in your sexual history, it's time to reclaim your sexual history. Share your pain with a friend or email us for assistance at bull@knightsofthe21stcentury.com.

Let's talk about the pleasure the penis provides and how to be responsible with our choices. Learning how to maintain a balance between pleasure and responsibility is the key to understanding and guiding your sexuality. There is a statistic that has often been quoted among sex researchers. On a survey, which asked men if they had ever masturbated, 99.9% stated that they have and the other 0.1% were probably liars. Whether or not this is true, many of you have already, or will at some future time choose to touch your penis at a level of stimulation that will cause you to have an orgasm and release semen. Whether you do this or not, it is also likely that you will have what is called a "wet dream" and release semen while sleeping. The reality is that while you sleep, you will get several erections a night. An erection occurs when blood rushes into your penile tissue causing it to be stimulated for the purpose of a sexual release. How you respond to this desire defines whether you control your sexuality or your sexuality controls you.

I'm going to tell you what I, Roy, have told many men in counseling over the years. When your blood flow is going to your penis, there's a good chance your penis will override your thinking brain. It is very important to think about your sexuality and to establish within yourself ahead of time what the manly thing is to do about your sexual stimulation *before* you get to a certain level of sexual arousal. Now, this does not mean that there are times when you can't stop yourself, giving yourself permission to be irresponsible. What it does mean is that you should recognize how powerful your pleasure-seeking impulses can be and the need to be careful about putting yourself in situations where you must directly confront their power. You can always stop yourself from following through on your sexual impulses. You will not explode. Run, do math problems, take a cold shower, call a friend – it will help!

The *Bible* teaches us that God created our sexuality as a gift to us. There-fore, He isn't surprised by the pleasure-seeking power of it. In fact, the yearning that comes with wanting to complete the sex act is a metaphor that God used to describe His yearning for a relationship with us. So, when you experience the desire for sexual release, it is no more powerful than God's desire to have a relationship with you. That's how powerful He feels about walking in a relationship with you daily. Pretty awesome, huh?! The *Bible* is filled with stories of individuals who used their sexual-ity in ways that were wrong, and hurt themselves and others as a result. One story which depicts how sexuality was handled in the right way is the story of the young man, Joseph. Joseph was good-looking, and the wife of a man named Potiphar wanted to have sex with him. Genesis 39:10 states, "She spoke to Joseph day after day. But he told her he wouldn't make love to her. He didn't even want to be with her." Thinking in ways that God would want him to, Joseph knew that such behavior was sup-posed to occur with one woman, the woman to whom he was married. He also would likely have begun responding with an erection, as a result of Potiphar's wife showing him some skin and touching him. Having thought about his standards *before* he was sexually stimulated, he knew that to hang around on the edge of sexual desire made it more likely that he would choose to have a sexual relationship with her, violating God's command and his own ethics, so he left the situation quickly and did not mess around with it.

It is okay to enjoy the sexual parts of yourself and the pleasurable feeling that orgasms bring, whenever they occur. God set it up that way. What is not ever right is for you to violate God's intentions for how this amazingly pleasurable aspect of yourself is used. So, you need to continue to keep your head in the game and ask Him to empower you; this will ensure that you will guide this area of your life in manly ways. It would have been much easier if God had created our sexuality with an on/off switch. The reality is, we have been given a dimmer switch and the chemical, testos-terone, that creates our sexual desire gets released into our bloodstream and is reabsorbed regularly. We can encourage the release of this chemi-cal by how we think and what we look at. So, we not only have some control over our sexual behavior, but also over our sexual desires, by how we manage this area of ourselves.

Our manhood is often determined by doing what is tough. The truth is that many of you have looked ahead and have read this section early, which shows both by your interest and your awareness that it is important to you to learn how to manage this aspect of who you are. If you or your father have already messed up in this area, it's not too late. God is there to forgive you when you ask Him, and you can start over again by living life by being more sexually disciplined. What is important is that you keep God's end goal for your sexual expression in mind. He doesn't want you looking at sexually stimulating pictures or videos, or attaching your sexual expression to an object. You have to be careful with your use of the internet and any form of pornography. His desire is that you express yourself sexually in a relationship, with one woman to whom you are committed in marriage. Anything short of this cheats you, cheats her, and negatively influences your walk with God. May God bless your efforts to honor Him with this pleasurable, powerful, God-created force within you.

Manhood Discussion - Chapter 18

1. Fathers: Tell your son what you think he should know regarding his sexuality. Share with him how you learned about your sexuality.

2. Sons: Ask your dad two questions about the issue of sexuality. Choose two topics related to sexuality to discuss with him. Share some of the sex talk you hear from your peers.

3. Discuss how sex, love, and God interact. How do you both feel about the issue of sexual abuse?

4. Discuss the availability of sexual images within our culture, and the need to control sexual stimulation by thinking about your ethics regarding sexual issues ahead of time.

5. In the Song of Songs 7:1-9, Solomon writes,

> You are like a prince's daughter. Your feet in sandals are so beautiful. Your graceful legs are like jewels. The hands of a skilled worker must have shaped them. Your navel is like a round bowl that always has mixed wine in it. Your waist is like a mound of wheat that is surrounded by lilies. Your two breasts are lovely. They are like two young antelopes. Your neck is smooth and beautiful like an ivory tower. Your eyes are like the pools of Heshbon by the gate of Bath Rabbim. Your nose is like the towering mountains of Lebanon that face the city of Damascus. Your head is like a crown on you. It is as beautiful as Mount Carmel. Your hair is as smooth as purple silk. I am captured by your flowing curls. You are so beautiful! You please me so much! You are so delightful, my love! You are as graceful as a palm tree. Your breasts are as sweet as the freshest fruit. I said, 'I will climb the palm tree. I'll take hold of its fruit.' May your breasts be as sweet as the fruit on the vine. May your breath smell like the tastiest apples. May your lips be like the finest wine.

How do these *Bible* verses apply to the manhood journey? Why did God put these verses in the *Bible*?

War Horse

19

Ah yes, the War Horse! A chapter driven by the burning passion deep in the belly of my 5-foot, 8-inch, 157 pound body! If it were my call, I would simply say, be a War Horse, you sissy, and end the chapter. However, my mentor decided for me that no one would have the slightest clue what I was talking about and instructed me to keep writing past that single sentence. So, you can thank my mentor for this chapter, gentlemen, for if he hadn't pressed me to write more, you would stumble through this chapter, dazed and confused.

Believe it or not, there was once a time when war was not fought by men in tanks or holding rifles, but instead, men on horseback with shields and swords. Battle zones were much more compact and chaotic. Hundreds, if not thousands, of men would barrel down on one another preparing for hand-to-hand, in-your-face, don't-blink-or-you'll-die warfare. Man soon realized that he could aid his team with a tool far surpassing any other – the War Horse, gigantic creatures decked out in armor, ridden by fearless warriors, ready to obliterate any man who stood in their way.

If I were to ask you to pick one and only one adjective to describe the War Horse, what would you say? Brave, intimidating, powerful, steadfast, strong, and fearless were a few answers that I heard from the friends I asked. Well, these are all great adjectives to describe these excellent war machines, but none of them are the *best* word to use when describing these majestic stallions. Meek, that's right, meek, is the adjective that describes the War Horse better than anything else. At some point along our time line, some clown decided that the term meek meant weak and that anyone who was meek probably looked like the gym class nerd with his goofy glasses and poorly parted hair, with his shirt tucked into his underwear, being pelted in the face repeatedly with dodge balls from the jocks in class who towered over him, all while flexing their gigantic biceps and displaying their abdominal sections. However, this is not the case. Meek never has and never will mean weak. Meekness is a characteristic that each man should strive to perfect. One of the definitions of meek is enduring injury with patience and without resentment, which can be interpreted as *having strength in reserve*. War Horses were the strongest tools of the knight. These horses towered over their enemies and had brute strength and fearless dispositions. They could easily kill any man who got in their path. However, what was considered even more important than this animal's brute strength was its meekness, or strength in reserve. These horses were able to stand fast in a chaotic battle with hundreds of men throwing spears and swinging swords at their riders. Instead of panicking, bucking, and eventually dumping their riders to the ground where they would no longer be at an advantage, these horses held their ground. They were obedient to their riders and were not easily startled. By the same token, they were never overly aggressive. These horses knew their power and strength, but more importantly, knew how to contain this power and use it only when absolutely necessary.

A man is like a War Horse. He understands his tremendous strength (whether it be physical, mental, or spiritual) and uses it with maturity and great wisdom. A male without the mental toughness to control his strength will simply lash out at those who oppose him. He defines his power from a limited perspective and impulsively uses it at a moment's notice. These males are not meek, but *weak*. It takes a courageous, steadfast man to understand that he must use his power only when absolutely necessary. He does not easily frighten when in danger; he does not run away, leaving his brothers behind; he stands fast, ready for battle. At the same time, he also understands that running headlong into battle, screaming at the top of his lungs and chasing about aimlessly, is of no help either. Instead, he marches into battle, ready for whatever evil is thrown his way; he stands his ground, digs in, and prepares for all-out war.

Brandon Lawrence was a close friend of mine while I was in high school. A massive creature with hands the size of frying pans, a beard which I am positive he grew in third grade and a back you could land a 747 on, he was intimidating to say the least. Being a man of God, Brandon knew that he had gifts as an athlete and that God had allowed him to reach great heights in sports. Brandon decided to join our high school wrestling team in his junior year and immediately began proving himself as a tremendous force on the mats. Brandon went on to wrestle in college and also coaches those who are looking for advice at our local gym. Being the massive dude that he is, Brandon could have chosen to dive headfirst into every one of his matches, ready to rip his opponent's head off and add it to his trophy case. However, Brandon knew the strategy of wrestling and understood that he must be meek. He would rarely, if ever, jump straight into a match without first sizing up his opponent and getting a feel for his strengths and weaknesses. On the other hand, Brandon would never just back down and simply avoid confrontation during his time on the mat. He would approach each match with his strength in reserve. He would use his strength when it was needed, but would use skill and judgment first. Brandon knew that only when he absolutely needed that last burst of explosive power and strength would he indeed use it. He was like the War Horse: calm, cool, collected, ready at any time to spring into action, with the understanding that he would use his brute strength only when absolutely necessary.

I encourage you to act like the War Horse. Whatever great gift God has given you, start holding it in reserve. You do not need to flaunt your talents and strengths, instead, use them with wise judgment. On the battlefield of life, you do not want to be showing your strongest weapon for the enemy to easily see; keep it in reserve until it's time to cut your opponent down and be victorious.

"The Holy Spirit led Jesus into the desert. There the devil [Satan] tempted him" (Matthew 4:1). As men, we are in the most danger and are more likely to make a wrong choice when we are alone. It has been said that we are only as sick as our secrets. Satan, the enemy, went about his attempts to destroy Jesus in a pattern that he will use against us to this day. "After 40 days and 40 nights of going without eating, Jesus was hungry"

(Matthew 4:2). The devil [Satan] tempted Jesus to prove He is the Son of God, and told Jesus, "… 'If you are the Son of God, tell these stones to become bread'" (Matthew 4:3), which was a temptation of pleasure. Standing at the highest point of the temple in the holy city, the devil told Jesus, "'If you are the Son of God, … throw yourself down'" (Matthew 4:5-6). In this way, Jesus was offered the power over a kingdom. From a very high mountain, the devil showed Jesus "… all the kingdoms of the world and their glory" (Matthew 4:8). The devil told Jesus, "'If you bow down and worship me, … I will give you all of this'" (Matthew 4:9). "Jesus said to him, 'Get away from me Satan! It is written, 'Worship the Lord your God. He is the only one you should serve.' Then the devil left Jesus. Angels came and took care of him" (Matthew 4:10-11). To this day, Satan tempts us to sin in different ways. Most people are aware of the temptation to obtain power. It has been said, "Power tends to corrupt, and absolute power corrupts absolutely. Great men are almost always bad men."[1] Power can be of a political nature which controls others, an economic nature which controls financial resources, or a physical nature which controls one's physical well-being. God promises to help us avoid temptation. That's what a line in the Lord's Prayer is all about: "… lead us not into temptation, …" (Matthew 6:13; *Bible* - King James Version). When we pray those words, we are asking that God would help us avoid or overcome temptation.

Instead of giving in to an unhealthy need for power, Jesus demonstrated that He would live up to His "Blessed are those who are free of pride" (Matthew 5:5) standards. He was strong and centered; He did not have to flaunt His power. His ability to be centered came from His understanding to God the Father's presence within Him and His desire to do God's will. He knew that "Since God is on our side, who can be against us?" (Romans 8:31). This gave Him the power to say "No" to cheap substitutes that He was already given by God. We can choose to build our strengths on a relationship with God. By placing our faith in Jesus Christ and walking with Him the way God designed us to, we know that we can conquer the challenges we face and achieve success in life. Ephesians 2:10 states, "God made us. He created us to belong to Christ Jesus. Now we can do good things. Long ago God prepared them for us to do." As Christ's War

1 John Emerich Edward Dalberg Acton in a letter to Bishop Mandel Creighton – 1887.

Horses, let's enter life's battle with an understanding of who our Master is, and take on the fight to change the world, starting with ourselves.

Manhood Discussion - Chapter 17

1. As a man, discuss your response to being compared to a War Horse. What does it mean for you to live your life in meekly ways and keep your strength in reserve? Which of your personal characteristics give you the strength that you need to deal with life?

2. Identify a time in your life when you acted with strength. How did that feel? How did the situation turn out?

3. Discuss the three ways (pleasure, popularity, and power) Jesus was tempted. How are you tempted in the same ways? Do you believe that you are more likely to hurt yourself and others when you allow yourself to become isolated and do not have relationships with people who hold you accountable (accountability relationships)?

4. Romans 8:31 states, "What should we say then? Since God is on our side, who can be against us?" Discuss this *Bible* verse and its implications to the manhood journey.

How Do We Decide What Is Right And Wrong?

Many people from this era have decided that choosing between right and wrong is not that important. What matters in life is not about being honest and holding oneself accountable for one's actions, but simply getting ahead. If you need to cheat on a test to pass the class, do it. If you need to lie on a timesheet to pay off your overdue bills, go for it. If you have to undermine another person to get a spot on the team, don't hesitate. Ever since I was a boy, the notion of getting ahead in life was expressed in brilliant flashing lights everywhere I looked. My teachers would tell me to do whatever it took to achieve an excellent future, my coaches told me to never let an opponent stand in my way, and news reports have shared countless stories about someone achieving great heights by any means necessary. While these men and women had great intentions with their advice about life, they were missing an important part of the equation: Doing so in a truthful, honest manner.

As our nation becomes increasingly liberal, we are continually challenged to provide reasons for our beliefs while being pressured to submit to the ways of the world. Some of what we define as right and wrong is founded clearly in the scriptures and in the Ten Commandments. Other rules or Biblical interpretations are much more subjective; they are based on culture, denomination, or the personality needs of the individual making the decisions. Let's consider the issue of drinking alcohol. My uncle, my coauthor on this book, has never had a drink of alcohol in his life. He knows that alcohol caused trouble in the lives of some of his relatives and as some people abstained in the Old Testament, so does he. He doesn't disagree with me about the use of alcohol in moderation. However, he and I agree that people should be of age; they should not drive under the influence, and should beware of a genetic predisposition to alcoholism.

There are three parts to every *Homo sapiens* with an XY chromosome pair. The first part is a constant. That person is a male. The other two parts vary widely. Is he a man? Is he Christian? These XY-chromosome individuals vary widely. We have males who are nothing more than that – Males! They have not yet achieved manhood. We have Christian males who have accepted Christ, but have not yet grown in their relationship with Him. We have some non-Christian men who, in my opinion, can often be easier to relate to than some immature Christian males. Lastly, we have what everyone reading this book should strive to be: the Christian *man*. This is the guy who has his act together in many aspects of his life, and is actively confronting the areas in which he needs to improve. Backtracking a bit, let's take a minute to differentiate between a man and a male. My uncle once told me that the easiest way to tell whether the person in front of you is a man or a male is this: A male measures himself by what is between his legs; a man measures himself from within.

You see, right and wrong can't be found through Biblical principles alone. God added an asterisk when He wrote down His Word. He told us that, first, we need to follow God and listen to His Word. Everything in the *Bible* is true, but not all that is true is found in the *Bible*. For example, each man has four chambers in his heart which need to beat in a certain rhythm for his heart to work effectively. This fact is not found in the *Bible*. How do we live according to truth when much of what is true may not be found in the *Bible*? First, we must follow what we know is true and what the *Bible* states. That alone is enough to keep us busy for a lifetime. Mark 4:25 states, "If you have something, you will be given more. If you have nothing, even what you have will be taken away from you." I take this to mean that if we have been handed the light (knowledge of God through the scriptures) and make proper use of it, we will be given more, and will understand more as a result of God's guidance. But if we choose to ignore what has been given to us, we will be set aside. This is a serious consequence when you consider that our goal is to achieve manhood. Secondly, we must choose to become men who walk daily with Jesus. In John 14:6, Jesus states, "I am the way, the truth, the life." It is this daily walk, following in Christ's footsteps, that will help us find the truth that is outside scripture.

In 2 Corinthians 10:3, God tells us that we live in the world, but are not *of* the world; this means that there are a lot of ways that God wants us to be which don't fit with what the world teaches or expects. We live in a world where being a Christian does not necessarily mean you are a popular man. At the same time, we are following a God who expects us to mature in our manhood. We must be capable of providing for our loved ones and standing up to our enemies, in addition to constantly searching for knowledge and truth. In order to accomplish these important manly goals, we cannot simply *be* in a relationship with God; we must *mature* in our relationship with Him and want His guidance. Jesus wanted us to come to Him in childlike faith (this is where many Christians stay, as they find themselves very comfortable here), but He expects us to take it one step further and progress to the maturity of a saint who can put his life on the line for what matters most. Unfortunately, I have seen many Christian males do very destructive things that harm themselves and those around them. They have ignored their God-given calling, disrespected His guidance, and pretty much spit on His message. In contrast, I have seen many strong men who have not yet found God. But, there is nothing more powerful than when you combine a Christian and a man. These men are the most powerful and courageous Bull Elephants.

Now that we are on the same page, let's turn our attention to the main question of the chapter. How do we determine what is right and what is wrong, as Christian men? There are two ways that humans determine right from wrong. The first way is one that is not ingrained in our DNA and is not a God-given attribute: Societal Rightness. You see, Societal Rightness is something that has developed over time. With each passing decade, it becomes a more dominant force on the formation of our decisions. It can conflict with the truth that God expects as part of manhood. Societal Rightness has its place and, if limited properly, can be a helpful tool. Society is wrong when it implies that there is nothing wrong with doing whatever we want, whenever we want. On the other hand, society is being truthful when it tells us that murder is wrong. Society overvalues pleasure as a motivator and tends not to confront older males who act as if it is okay to hurt others by neglecting them. Society does not teach what manhood is, the value of adopting high standards, the importance of knowing God, or the significance of family life. There is a disastrous time in our history, during the Nazi reign in Germany, when murdering Jews was seen as okay. So, what sits in the gap between what society tells us is right and our knowledge that what we are being told is actually wrong?

The answer is us! With the help of God, we can look at what society says is either right or wrong and find out the actual truth. In a culture of compromise where "everything goes" and the rules are constantly changing, we need to walk closely with Christ in order to figure out how truth is defined outside of the *Bible*, as well as to apply the truth that is found in the *Bible* to our daily lives. Loving others is God's command. How to put His command into action is what we need to figure out. Sometimes, confrontation is done in anger, which is destructive to both you and the person you are accusing. At another time, with the right motivation, it is a loving act. Talking about your anger in the right tone, with God's help, and working through your aggression in an appropriate way, may actually help someone.

A true man understands that a firm belief in Jesus takes precedence when making the right choices in life. Yes, our Societal Rights can sometimes help us know that it is wrong to cheat on a test or avoid helping a friend when we promised we would. But, we need to filter our view of what is right through what God tells us in the *Bible* and what His Spirit tells us, as we walk daily with Him. We can become strong warriors for Christ in this battle of life if we understand what is right and seek empowerment from God to do it. Many Christian males are not reliable, lash out at their loved ones, and are scared, shallow men. They lack a man's internal strength to do what is right. It is only those Christians who truly understand that God wants them to live a life for Him while being accountable for their daily actions, helping those in need, and keeping themselves in check, who are really living as a Christian *and* as a man.

111

A choice to follow the *Bible* and its view of God determines a lot of our life for us. Having the right relationship with God is the most important thing in life. The concept that two hydrogen atoms and one oxygen atom make water is a truth that we discovered through science. Mathematicians have proven that a triangle must have three angles equaling 180 degrees. However, the central and most important truth for us, is that who we are and what we can become is based on our faith in Christ. A true man knows what is right and stands by his principles. He looks toward the Bulls in his life for guidance; he also seeks guidance from Jesus, follows the path God designed for him, and will not have wandered off into the dark shadows of wrong-doing.

No one is perfect, which is why Christ had to die for us on the cross; even when we know what is wrong, we find ourselves doing it anyway. In Romans 7:18-20, Paul, a follower of Jesus, talks about how hard it can be to do what is right. Discovering the truth, even when it is hidden, is a lot easier than applying it. As Paul shows us, our natural instinct to sin is a constant struggle. Jesus' life reiterates this concept, as He had many interactions with religious figures who knew the *Bible* in their heads, but lost its true message in their hearts. Jesus had to confront the lack of spiritual maturity in the religious figures He interacted with and, as young men, we face this same type of confrontation. We must make a decision about the existence of God for ourselves and how we will overcome our destructive sinful nature, in order to apply the truth to our manly walk. As we continue to grow, there will be times when we go back to our immature ways. What is *not* okay is to choose to have a relationship with God and to become a man, but to remain immature!

Manhood Discussion - Chapter 20

1. As you both look at your lives at this point in time, identify three choices that you believe are the right thing to do and three that you believe would be wrong. What are you basing your answers on?

2. Why do you think some of the non-Christian men we meet are more likeable than some of the Christian men we know? Identify three characteristics that demonstrate the maturity of a Christian man's faith.

3. Identify three Biblical concepts or principles that can help you with life. Identify three facts about life that are not discussed in the *Bible*. What do you think about the concept that the *Bible*'s central truth is based on who God is and how to have a relationship with Him?

4. Identify three ideas that you believe the culture supports which do *not* help you in life. Identify three concepts/ideas that society supports which you agree with. A man determines for himself which ideas support manhood and which ones don't.

5. Romans 7:24 states, "What a terrible failure I am! Who will save me from this sin that brings death to my body?" What does this *Bible* verse mean in relation to this chapter? Share how you feel when you choose not to do the right thing, even though you know what it is.

What Does A Man Do When He Is Wrong?

Now, to answer this question, my answer will be based purely on a guess; I think that if you give any male the choice between cutting off his left leg or admitting he is wrong, he will most likely give you his left leg. This is not true for a man. Despite man's early historical choices to sin, the idea of choosing to do what is morally right continues to be held in high regard. Even Adam, the first man to walk the earth, was afraid and naked, when he left God's way (Genesis 3:10). Since that time, males have had issues with being wrong and even when we realize we're wrong, we hate to admit it. Males are born to be competitive. As a result, they hate to lose. When a male admits he is wrong, he feels less powerful. A man, in contrast, has a structure inside him that is strong enough to deal with this unpleasant reality. To some males, admitting that they are wrong is one of the most embarrassing and painful things in life. A man, however, sees his imperfections as "just the way it is" and has thought about emotional and spiritual solutions for his imperfections.

We all know that males hate to be wrong and to be beat. However, what males hate even more than losing a battle is losing a battle to a *woman*! In my attempt to encourage you to admit when you are wrong, I will tell you about a woman who is an expert at admitting she is wrong. Now gentleman, if she can do this, and you can't, it shows me that she is more of a man than you'll ever be.

My mother is a "man" in her own right. She has more testicular fortitude than most males out there. She has sacrificed more time to a greater cause than anyone I know. Close to 30 years ago, she dove into a newly-formed business that is dedicated to helping others, and has stuck with it ever since. Now, as the second-in-command, she handles most of the important matters that go on in the business which requires a lot of meetings, both in groups and one-to-one. Every day, all day, my mother has the difficult task of telling her employees when they are wrong, figuring out when they are right, and deciding how to do the right thing. She does it kindly and makes certain that she does her best not to offend anyone. When I was living at home, my mom, my father and I would sit down at the dinner table at the end of the day to discuss the adventures of the day. At some point, my mom and I would get into an argument over something trivial and enter the battlefield of disagreement. We would each present our point of view, throw in counterpoints, and wait in angst for a witty rebuttal. Meanwhile, my father sat in silence holding back bouts of laughter. Neither of us ever got upset, because most of our arguments were silly and held no merit other than to prove the other wrong. Luckily for me, most of the arguments we got into were on topics that I know a bit more about: sports, history, fishing, more sports, hiking, spitting, climbing trees, you know, manly topics! Needless to say, most nights I ended up victorious and paraded around the kitchen like a true champion. She ended up smarter because she had learned about a new area of life, and got to know me better.

My mom accepted defeat, laughed it off, and continued living. She didn't get caught up in the fight, reminisce about it, or seek vengeance on me during the next argument. She simply accepted the fact that she lost, admitted it, learned from it, and went on with her day as if nothing happened. She has *perfected* the art of being wrong. Also, I am certain that once she reads this part of my book, she'll be waiting with an argument in attempt to prove me wrong; to that I say, bring it on, Mother dearest! So, to conclude the first part of this chapter, let's all start to learn how to admit when we are wrong, and realize that taking ownership of these times is a strength. As my mother has so perfectly proved, you will not die, face execution, or lose your very being when you are proven wrong; instead, keep on living with your head held high.

Now, when embarking on a journey to learn how to accept it, when you are wrong, you must also understand what to do when this happens. A male has several options when confronted with being wrong. He can lie by telling others that he was right. He can walk away angry and hold a grudge. He can admit to others that he was wrong, but think that he was not really wrong, or he can admit to himself that he was wrong, but not tell anyone. The male has developed plenty of ways to deal with being wrong, many of which allow him to avoid facing the situation like a man.

On the other hand, a man has only one option: he admits his wrongs, embraces them, apologizes, and moves on. In fact, it isn't even an option because the term "option" implies having choices. A man must handle being wrong in one way. He embraces his wrong-doings and uses them as an opportunity to grow. He does not hang on to his failed attempts at being right nor does he try to get revenge on those who know more than he does. True men see the concept of being wrong as a gift and use it as a further step toward manhood. You see, every time a man is shown to be wrong, he understands that it is another opportunity to grow. When he is proved to be wrong, he looks inward, acknowledges his mistakes and learns from them. A true man does not make the same mistake twice; he learns from his previous errors. When a knight makes a mistake or chooses the wrong strategy in the midst of a battle, he can find himself missing an arm, a leg, or a head. Lucky for you, most of the issues that you are wrong about won't cost you your life. So, when you are, in fact, wrong, learn from it, grow as a result of it, and make sure you don't end up like the Black Knight from Monty Python: armless, legless and eventually headless.

When I ran for Coach Harrison, I learned to trust his judgment without question. However, there was a time, early on in my track career, that I thought I knew how to run track better than he did and was willing to prove him wrong. Before one particular race, Coach told me to make sure not to try to out-sprint my opponent until the last possible second. He explained that if I wanted to win the race, I should simply tail my opponent and let him set the pace until the final stretch, then open up my stride and make an all-out sprint for the finish line (even though an 800-meter dash is already a sprint to begin with). Now, Coach is an excellent Bull, as we already know. Being a Bull, he understands the importance of not protecting me from failure; he let me run the race the way I felt I should run it. I got whooped in the Open 8 and cost our team a few points at that track meet. After my race, I went over to Coach, told him I was wrong and he was right, and from that day forward, I ran the way he told me to. I won a lot more races that year, thanks more to his strategy than my speed. In order to succeed, I had to first admit that I was wrong, and then change my strategy.

Coach proved he was right and I learned through making the mistake of running the race my way instead of his. Once I learned the hard way that he knew much more about race strategy than I did, I had a choice to make. Would I own my distorted thinking and grow, or would I stay the same? Heck, I hadn't even known there was a strategy to running a race; I just figured you ran until you crossed the line! Because I was able to face the reality of what happened in that situation, I was able to listen to his instructions about race strategy and started beating opponents who were much faster than I was. I learned to run smarter, not faster. If, instead, I had remained block-headed and ignored the fact that I was wrong, I would not have experienced the running success that I did.

We must learn the secret behind my mom's ability to acknowledge that she is wrong, while also being humble at the same time. Her secret to figuring out when she is wrong is that she is dedicated to the Christian squat of reading her *Bible* daily. Through this choice she acknowledges that there is a power beyond herself that is a measure for right and wrong. 2 Timothy 3:16 states, "God has breathed life into all of Scripture. It is useful for teaching us what is true. It is useful for correcting our mistakes. It is useful for making our lives whole again. It is useful for training us to do what is right." Expecting that you may be wrong is a major part of the battle against the parts of our sinful nature that want life to go our own way.

When we accept our capacity to be wrong, the beauty of believing in Christ is that it makes dealing with being wrong much easier. You see, we cannot pay for our latest sin; we are too busy dealing with the consequences of the last six, seven, eight, or more sins. 1 John 1:9 states, "But God is faithful and fair. If we admit that we have sinned, he will forgive us our sins. He will forgive every wrong thing we have done. He will make us pure." So when you are wrong, tell God, accept His forgiveness and believe Him when He states that because of your faith in Christ, He's got your back.

Manhood Discussion - Chapter 21

1. List three times that you have been wrong. What happened as a result? How hard was it for you to own that you were wrong and acknowledge it to others? What is your response when you discover that you are wrong?

2. Describe four strengths that your mother has. Identify a weakness that you see in your mom. How hard is it for you to tell her that you love her? Men need to encourage others, and this means complimenting them. If it's possible and if it's true, tell your mom one of the ways that you appreciate her during the next week.

3. Identify a time when your mom showed testicular fortitude. A relationship with a strong woman is a very valuable asset in life. List several times that your mother was there to help you out.

4. Discuss *Bible* verse 2 Timothy 3:16: "God has breathed life into all of Scripture. It is useful for teaching us what is true. It is useful for correcting our mistakes. It is useful for making our lives whole again. It is useful for training us to do what is right." What are the implications that scripture has on the manhood journey?

5. Discuss *Bible* verse 1 John 1:9: "But God is faithful and fair. If we admit that we have sinned, he will forgive us our sins. He will forgive every wrong thing we have done. He will make us pure."

When Good Bulls Go Bad

22

Up to this point, I have been saying to all of you who are willing to listen that the men in our lives who are given the title of Bull Elephant seem to be just shy of perfect. These men have learned from many of their mistakes, and by the time we see them as Bulls, they appear to hardly ever screw up. They have turned their many failures into strengths and no longer let their character flaws overshadow their God-given call to lead. What was once a weak link, defined as failure, is now a shortcoming or inadequacy that they have used to grow in their manhood journey. They are willing to share their lack of perfection with us, and don't dominate with a "see what I can do" attitude. Instead of using their position to brag to us, they would rather help us. The truth is, anyone who is able to run long and fast in the here and now once walked on weak and shaky legs. Every man is bound to fail, mess up, screw up, botch up, or do something wrong, somewhere, sometime, somehow. We've discussed what happens when we screw up, but what do we do when the men we hold high in our hearts do something that goes completely against their character?

Maturing young men collapse back into their maleness on a daily basis as they witness the Bull Elephants who are their role models doing wrong. These Bulls are held to such high standards by the young men in their lives that when the Bulls behave in unmanly ways or make choices that are wrong, young guys do one of two things. They break down because it destroys their belief in these great men; they may collapse back into being males themselves. When these young men witness their Bulls messing up big time, they then think that the wrong behaviors they are observing are okay, causing them to define manhood in male ways. They internalize these distorted thoughts and bring these types of male traits into their toolbox of manhood thinking. They willingly place these male traits next to the tools of honesty, integrity, love, passion, and courage. They fail to see them as the character defects that they are.

A young man who is wise is able to fight through his disappointment, as those he has once trusted has failed big time. This young leader understands that even the biggest, strongest Bulls are merely men and can make mistakes. A man screws up; it's a fact of life and unfortunately when we achieve a Bull status, we can do the same. However, what a man does when he screws up determines if he is going to restore his manhood or remain a male. A young impressionable man needs to understand first that no one is perfect, no matter how much we look up to him. We can learn from our role models, but we also need to understand that we can't rely on them to be flawless. They are real men, and so our idealization of them needs to be controlled. We must understand and find forgiveness in our hearts; after all, come judgment day, it's not a jury decision, but rather the one true Judge who will determine a man's fate. Therefore, a young buck must press forward, accept his battle wound, wrap it up, and let it heal. Letting himself be harmed by another man's negative choices is to compound the tragedy.

One of the Bull Elephants in my life is my Uncle Paul, although he tells me that in his own eyes he is barely a Bull Chipmunk, if that. Uncle Paul is my dad's older brother, a quiet man who, like me, is extremely organized and clean. He never says much, but has a "noggin" filled with knowledge. His mind works like a bear trap; once information goes in, it never leaves. Uncle Paul served our country in Vietnam, a true act of valor in my eyes. He loves his family and puts me, his siblings, and those around him first, an equally courageous act. Last summer, my grandmother on my dad's side of the family, passed away: a sweet old lady with a heart of gold, a laugh that could melt even the most wicked of men, and a love for Jesus beyond most others in this world. Out of everyone in the family, Uncle Paul took her passing the hardest. A man with no real faith in God, he took her death as the end, not the beginning, and it absolutely crushed him. Trying to cope with her loss along with some serious medical struggles he was facing, he found himself slipping into a deep depression. Eventually, he turned to alcohol to cope with his overwhelming grief.

Now, here I was, at the age of 22, watching a man who was one of my top Bull Elephants crash and burn. What was I to do? I could turn my back on him, scold him for his slip-up, and scratch him off my list of Bulls, never allowing him back into the elite pack of men whom I hold high in my mind. *Or* I could understand that he was just human, bound to mess up at some point, love him unconditionally, offer him my support, and do my part in helping him through his pain. I knew the choices that he was making were wrong, but I also knew that he needed support if he was going to have a chance to bounce back and make wiser decisions. My uncle hit rock bottom about a week after I graduated from college. He was unable to attend my graduation party, as he was drinking and could not drive to our home. A few days later, he stopped answering his phone and email while he stayed cooped up in his house, drowning his sorrows one glass after another.

BUT, it was during this low point in life when he found the love of God, accepted Jesus into his heart, and began his adventure back to sobriety. It was at his lowest point in life that he truly showed me his desire to regain his Bull Elephant status. What did he do to show me his true Bull colors? He *tried*, one tough step at a time. Not just for himself, but for the love of his family, his love for me, and his new found love for Christ. You can compare it to anything in life that was challenging to you, and that's the type of battle my uncle had to combat every second of every day to work his way back into a normal life without alcohol. Now *that*, gentlemen, takes some massive quantities of testicular fortitude, courage, love, and drive. Uncle Paul showed me, his brother, his family, and God that he wasn't going down without a fight; he was willing to right his wrongs, and he would make up for the pain that he caused his loved ones.

This story has two sides. First off, I understood, as you must also, that even Bulls make mistakes. By loving him, respecting him, and offering my support, I stuck by him, even when he screwed up. After all, who is to say I won't screw up one day and need his unconditional support? By holding a grudge against him, judging him for his wrongdoing, and discarding him from my list of Bulls, I would be no better than him. Two wrongs never make a right, and abandoning a man who is in need of help is not a manly act. I could reach out to help him because I'm committed to becoming a man; I knew the direction that Jesus would want me to take, and I had the support of other men. On the other hand, my uncle proved his worth by fighting his battle internally and making certain that he did not short-circuit his road to recovery; instead, he threw on his suit of armor, picked up his shield and sword, mounted his War Horse, and marched headfirst into battle to get his life back. He used his faith in God to overcome the seemingly impossible. It is a great honor to be walking on the battlefield of life alongside this epic war hero, and to see his ability to fight his external war, as well as his internal war. I would gladly pick up my sword and march into the belly of the beast alongside my uncle, because I know that he willingly faced how he acted, acknowledged that it was wrong, and worked to change it.

I understand that we are not all blessed by having great men in our lives who slip, but eventually catch themselves. There are some men in this world who slip, only to fall flat on their faces and never get back up and fight. These men decide that their adversary is too large, too powerful, and too overwhelming to keep on fighting. They lay down their swords and shields and surrender. What do we do when these Bull Elephants take *themselves* off the list of Bulls? Our first priority, as future Bulls, is to encourage these fallen men to get back on their feet, adjust their armor, and keep fighting the good fight. However, there are times when some men choose not to press on; they hang up their manhood armor and cross over to the side of males. What now? We can write these men off, swear not to speak to them again, and cast a dark shadow over their images for all to see. Or we can be true men, or true young Bulls, ourselves. We can forgive them for their wrongdoings, pray for them, love them, and move on with our lives. We must decide not to follow them and show our strength by choosing a better way. A male who has truly given up on himself, harming you in the process, does not care about your opinion any longer. By getting caught up in another man's wrongdoings we are hurting both ourselves and our Savior.

For you to get caught up with another man's wrong deeds is causing him no lack of sleep. He has written off what you have decided is right; he no longer cares about what you (or anyone else) think. You see, failure that is not dealt with can cause a person to become hard and bitter. However, as you toss and turn at night, with sadness in your heart, confusion and anger regarding the Bull who is letting you down, you are only causing yourself harm. By holding on to what he has done, you have chosen to add to his harm by harming yourself. Let go, move on, and understand that if you don't forgive him, you are letting this male win another battle over you. Be a true man, start earning your Bull Elephant title and stay on your path, fighting for your team. Don't let another man's screw-ups drag you to the enemy's side along with him.

Let's discuss what we do when a Bull in our lives doesn't do exactly what we believe should be done. He doesn't do something clearly wrong, but may just express his manhood differently than we expect. In other words, what happens when there are gray issues which begin to cloud the once black and white relationship between two men? Remember Shane? Well, this gym rat decided he was going to open a sports ministry geared towards Mixed Martial Arts (MMA), boxing, and wrestling. The gym flourished and was able to attract members who came in looking to learn how to fight and left with the knowledge of the power of the Lord and a greater understanding of how to be better people. Shane was excellent at leading these lost souls toward the light, as everyone looked up to this guy as a great leader. He was understanding, but firm, never backed down from anything, and told it how it was. If you screwed up, he would let you know and make sure you corrected your errors. I volunteered my free time to help Shane around his gym, as I saw what he was doing as a great act of kindness and selflessness from a humble servant of God.

About three years into the development of Shane's gym, many of the members started becoming frustrated, as they felt Shane had lost track of what was important and had become engulfed in other issues. First off, we need to look at the chapter on right and wrong again and determine if this is a scenario where there is truly a right and wrong, or if it is simply a case of two people not seeing eye to eye. I could have gone along with the group, talked behind Shane's back, and simply guessed at what his real motives were, *or* I could talk to him (look back at the chapter on communication) man to man. After a brief discussion with Shane, it turned out that what people were saying was partially true, from my perspective, and that he and I didn't agree on what the priorities should be. Now, when dealing with a sports ministry, or a ministry of any kind, there is a very delicate balance that needs to be maintained to keep it running smoothly. Shane was not completely out of line in his thinking, but those who looked up to him as a steadfast War Horse with absolutely zero flaws thought his new priorities were causing the gym to run less smoothly. In this situation, I needed to accept that Shane, being a man, naturally has flaws.

After discussing this delicate matter with Shane, we came to the conclusion that we, in fact, did not see eye to eye. Here is where I had a choice to make. I had this solid Bull Elephant whom I viewed as an older brother; a man who I had never seriously disagreed with up to this point, and he was choosing to emphasize things that put a sour taste in my mouth. Shane is a rather young Bull Elephant, but a wise one, nonetheless. He didn't just teach me lessons about weight-lifting, but about manhood as well. He was always there for me, and for my family and helped lead me closer to Christ than any other individual in my life.

At this point, I had two options: limit Shane's influence in my life or handle the situation like a man. In this area of life, we needed to get to the point where we could agree to disagree and still respect each other. Instead of completely shutting Shane out and disregarding him as a Bull, I instead *communicated* my disagreement with him, *listened* to his side of the story, came to the conclusion that he and I could not agree, and in the end, we continued to be good friends.

As young men, we will have opinions that conflict with the opinions of our Bull Elephants, even as each of us are motivated to honor God. During times like this, Bulls have, in their maturity, learned to look at each other and say "we'll agree to disagree." Disagreeing in this way respects each man's viewpoint while placing the value of the relationship above any minor disagreement. Our Bull Elephants are not perfect and we must understand this in order to truly see these Bulls for what they are: Servants of God. No one is perfect, and every Bull has his flaws. By loving and respecting these Bulls, flaws included, we can develop a strong character and be Bulls ourselves. God created us to be perfect and yet not all-powerful. We, in our humanity, as a result of Adam's choice to sin, are not perfect or grand enough to be God. So, how can we hold a grudge against a man who is displaying a quality that holds him short of perfection, when we ourselves are not perfect either?! Demeaning a man when he slips up and not showing him God's grace demonstrates that you are not yet ready to be a leader and haven't fully learned how to deal with your own imperfections.

King David was described as a man after God's own heart (Acts 13:22). As a powerful spiritual leader, David lost his Bull status by having sex with Bathsheba, another man's wife. Compounding his sin, he also killed Bathsheba's husband to prevent the discovery of his affair (2 Samuel 11). If you read Hebrews 11, the men who are described as performing great deeds all periodically fell out of their Bull status. Bull Elephant status is a state of being, not a once and done achievement. Once you attain manhood, you must continue to grow and remain vigilant.

The secret to getting past the failures of others who we respect is to take in what they teach us and compare it to God's message for us. Our trust, despite our love for these Bulls, must always be centered on God's love, as He is the ultimate Bull in our lives. God will never leave us or desert us (Deuteronomy 31:6), as our human Bulls may. There should be an ongoing process within us that utilizes the strength of the Bulls around us to encourage us to be like them in good ways. We should attribute the strengths we have observed in them as coming from God. God can help us maintain our Bull status. We can use the experiences and mistakes of other Bulls to teach us. Our ultimate success comes from taking in these life lessons, internalizing their messages, and turning our will over to Christ so that we can be empowered to continue our journey toward manhood. Any Bull will tell you that you need to depend on God and learn from your Bull Elephants. If we do this, we will be sad when a Bull drops down beside us on our path of life, but instead of being devastated, we will pursue our own true purpose.

Manhood Discussion - Chapter 22

1. Identify a couple of people whom you once looked up to as a role model and the ways that they let you down. What can you do to make it less likely that you will regress back toward your spandex male state?

2. What are your thoughts about manhood being a state, not a once and done achievement? Identify the areas in your life that if you are not careful, you can become immature and boy-like? What behaviors are indicators that you are stepping back toward maleness?

3. Have you chosen to use alcohol or drugs over the course of your lifetime? If yes, in what ways? How does the use of these substances relate to the manhood journey?

4. In 2 Samuel 11 of the *Bible,* read the story of David and Bathsheba. Discuss your ideas about how such a good man could go so wrong so quickly.

What Do We Do About God?

Whether we want to admit it or not, our need to make a faith choice is drilled into us, beginning with our first breath. If you were as fortunate as I was, you grew up in a family that filled itself with the love of Christ, cherishing God for all of His blessings. However, there are some males and men out there who have not been exposed to the tremendous power and love of God; they are walking through life without a true purpose. We must take a step back and consider their lost spiritual state before we can press forward. I believe that no man can become a true Christian man without contemplating the existence of God and His purpose. For a man to enter into the elite group of Bull Elephants, he must tackle the epic struggle of the existence of Christ on his own. Yes, his family's teachings can provide a solid foundation, but he alone must venture off into the world and come out on the other side with his own beliefs. So, while writing this chapter, I am putting us all on the same playing field. I don't care if you were brought up in a Christian home or have never heard Christ mentioned before this; we are all equals when we start reading this chapter. We will tackle these major questions together, with the assumption that we can all know more about how our world fits together spiritually. We will look at the evidence that is available to support our Christian faith. Because this topic is so important to a young man's well-being, I will not only give my own opinions on the matter; I will draw from men who are very credible in the fields of theology and philosophy, in hope of sharing some of their valuable opinions on the issue as well.

Before addressing the topic of God's existence, we must take some time to ask ourselves why Christ is absent from most young boys' lives, especially during their most stressful years: high school and college. Huston Smith, author of the book *Why Religion Matters*, discusses the role of God and religion in our society and the trend our nation is heading toward with regard to our Creator.[2] In *Why Religion Matters*, Smith points to several aspects of today's society that, for the most part, produce negative attitudes toward religion.[3] Growing up in a family that believed a relationship with Jesus Christ was the most important thing in life, I was always interested in this relationship and contemplated minimally the question of whether or not there is a "God." However, once I began college, my faith was tested as I saw firsthand the negative influences that Smith warns about.

Religion is a highly debatable topic, with thousands of differing interpretations. For this discussion, I will focus on Christianity, as it is my belief structure, and the faith system about which I know the most. To those who oppose Christianity, Christians are sometimes seen as a bunch of radical, right-wing nut jobs, who are so engulfed by their love for Jesus Christ that they neglect all other aspects of life. Unfortunately, at times, those who claim to believe and love Jesus do not reflect His love in their thinking and actions.

While there are several contributions to the negative light on religion, the media has, by far, been the greatest. A significant cause of this negativity is the coverage of the war on terror that has existed over time. On the surface, the multiple wars that America is part of are about standing up to terrorism. However, underneath the war on terrorism is the war on religion. The media will take any chance they have to show the total destruction of human morals and values through this war on religion. There are numerous stories of the atrocities that have happened on both sides, and they all point to religion, not terrorism. Religious individuals of any kind are painted in a negative light.

However, what the media has not shown us is the powerful positive effects of religion in the wars that America is fighting. In the book *Lone Survivor*,

2 Huston Smith, *Why Religion Matters* (New York: Harper Collins Publishers, 2006).
3 Smith, *Why Religion Matters*.

four Navy Seals are stranded in the wilds of Afghanistan and are quickly overtaken by a group of rebels. The author, Marcus Luttrell, tells in great detail, the horribly tragic way his fellow Seals died, one by one. But what Marcus also explains, in even greater detail, is the strength these men and their families back home had as they knew that this world was not "home," but merely a layover on the way to "home" or heaven. All three men, who died in combat, left this world knowing that they were heading home. Death did not intimidate these men, for their belief in God was so great that it trumped fear of death and dying. This book shows the kind of one-sidedness our media has when covering topics such as religion because these types of positive stories are never shared. The media does not talk about the wonderful contributions that religion brings to people, but focuses only on the kind of destruction religion brings on them.[4]

Along with the media, scientism is another great proponent of shutting down religion. From day one of their college experience, students are taught about the scientific method and all of its great powers. Through the scientific method, we are able to determine the cause and effect of many of the world's most perplexing problems. However, if something *(let's say "faith")* can't be measured, it's not worth talking about. The most significant aspect of Christianity is faith. Faith is defined as believing in something, even when there is no *evidence* that it exists. Scientism would suggest that there is no such thing as faith, as it cannot be measured. On top of this, scientism would ask how one can measure faith (which is unable to been seen, heard or felt) when faith itself is defined as having belief without seeing, hearing, or feeling. Scientism, believing in its own brilliance, ignores the fact that it is a faith system in and of itself. To scientism, any type of faith is seen as measuring nothing inside of nothing!

Both the media and scientism are portrayed within higher education as undeniably true. Higher education systems, as a whole, neglect religion all together. Classes, both upper and lower level, teach the scientific method, Darwinism, and Freud's beliefs, yet it is very rare that you can find a class that focuses on religion. Even in classes such as Psychology Seminar, Religiosity and Spirituality, the main focus is not on the fact that there

---

4 Marcus Luttrell, *The Eyewitness Account of Operation Redwing and the Lost Heroes of SEAL Team 10* (New York: Little, Brown and Company, 2007).

is a God, or that having a religion is truly important, but to question the importance of religion and the existence of God.

These facts, along with the ways that law and government impact our faith, greatly increase the chances that college students will neglect religion, rather than accept it. The college years (or young adulthood) are among the most impressionable and important years in life. It is during this time that you are able to figure out what you believe in, rather than to simply follow the beliefs of your parents, and then start down the path of your own adventure. To me, personally, it shows great character, determination, and steadfastness when a person is able to withstand the barrage of negativity against their belief system and continue to maintain them. Religion's biggest barrier is religion itself. Jesus told his followers that He did not want a religion, but a relationship, a *personal* relationship. Religion takes personal relationships, lumps them together, and creates an entity that is bound to fail. In order for Christianity to compete with scientism, the walls that separate Christians from others must come down, and start sharing the belief that "religion" should be between each person and God.

Now that we understand what it is that is pulling our young boys away from religion, we can turn toward questions that we, as Christians, might ask ourselves when contemplating the existence of God. The overall question of this chapter is whether or not God truly exists. To answer this, we must dig a little deeper and ask some questions that address less significant topics than the overall big picture of the existence of God. One of the first issues that comes to mind is the idea of filling our hearts with love in the same way that we fill our minds with knowledge. I will again turn to the writings of Huston Smith. Smith states that "all human beings have a God-shaped vacuum built into their hearts."[5] (Note: This was originally Pascal's thought in the 17th century.) He talks about life and people as being like a jigsaw puzzle with "a gaping hole at the puzzle's center."[6] So, we must ask ourselves, what are we filling our hearts with? There is no arguing that each human on this earth is striving to fill this missing puzzle piece with something, but what *is* that something?

---

5 Huston Smith, *Why Religion Matters* (New York: Harper Collins Publishers, 2006), p. 148.
6 Smith, *Why Religion Matters*, p. 148.

Since the second grade, I have wanted to become a psychologist, just like my father (*I even have the letter we wrote in class describing what we wanted to do when we grew up*). From that day forward, I have never looked back. I saw what my father did and all the lives that he touched. He has always instilled in me the fact that none of what he does is possible without the will and help of God. I have grown up devoting my life to God with the belief that all we do in this life is, ultimately, for Him. I have had many ups and downs, family issues, disappointments, and failures. But as I grow older, I understand that it is not always what we want; in the end, it is about His will, and being obedient to His Word.

However, there is another side to me that I battle with internally, literally *every single day*. I have a burning passion within me to write. If my words are passed on to one man or one million men, it makes no difference to me. All I care about is that I write down my ideas in hopes of being a shoulder to lean on or a beacon of light for just one individual. Here is where my angst came into play. I have a passion for psychology, but the more I learn to write, the further from psychology I find myself. What am I to do? I grew up believing that the only thing I wanted to do in this life was to sit down and listen to others, but, instead, I am finding myself doing most of the talking (*or writing, in this case*). I can't say what it is that grabs me about those who can write, and write well, but I have a deep-seated love and respect for those who can share their thoughts on paper. When I went to college, I started taking writing more seriously and became more critical of my writing. This seems to be one area that God has combined with an interest of mine which is turning out to be a meaningful puzzle piece.

I believe that God is ultimately the missing puzzle piece in all of our hearts, but the missing piece looks completely different to each individual. God is not just a "who" in our lives, but also a "where." To me, the missing puzzle piece is God. But what would this God-like missing piece look like? A summer with sleepless nights spent hovering over my computer, letting God's words flow through me, knowing that with each passing minute, I was losing more sleep as I had to be up early the next day to drive to work. The missing piece is not just "God" in the sense of His presence in my life, but finding God's will for my life. Each person needs to find their calling in life, and determine how that calling is to be used to fulfill God's will. Smith is exactly right when he tells us that we each have a missing puzzle piece. However, I believe he needs to further refine this statement by saying that it is not just God, Himself, that is missing (for He is there), but our willingness to submit to God's will for our lives. When we can find, within us, what God has called us to do, then, and only then, will the gap left by this missing puzzle piece be filled, and our heart-shaped puzzle will be complete.

So, we understand that there are forces out there, such as the media and higher education, that are preventing our young boys from finding truth. We also have discussed whether or not God is seen by each and every one of us. Now, let us turn this topic on its head and ask ourselves, how have we developed over time and how is God a part of that development? What kind of "self" do you think you were four or five years ago? What kind of "self" are you now, and how has it changed?

"Finally!" I told myself as my parents dropped me off at Elwell, the iconic symbol for incoming freshmen at Bloomsburg University, and the biggest dorm on campus. It's been 18 years of waiting to leave my hometown and venture off into the world by myself, to prove to myself that I can make it on my own, and find out what is beyond the narrow corridors of my high school. Looking back, I thought I had my act together. I believed that I was smart enough, knowledgeable, and could take on any challenge. I can see how much I've grown in the last few years: mentally, physically, spiritually, and emotionally. I want to treat this section more as a reflection than an issue of discussion – a reflection of the struggles and triumphs that turned me into the man I am today.

I have been one of the lucky few in this world to be surrounded by people who are just downright better at *life* than I am. Shane, with his spiritual wisdom, Marine Corps attitude, and brotherly love, has taught me more about honesty, integrity, and confidence than I could ever have imagined. My father, with all his wisdom, has shared his insights with me, and is molding me into a carbon copy of himself, currently shaping me into a Wisdom Biscuit, on my way, hopefully, to becoming a Wisdom Muffin. Coach Harrison taught me to be organized, determined, and above all, to live by this very important rule: Excuses are the nails in the house of failure. I have allowed myself to become vulnerable with them and let them teach me.

My "self" is viewed as a black hole. I take in my surroundings, listen carefully, take notes when appropriate, and use this knowledge to grow. When I find information that is valuable, I try to apply it to life in practical ways. I take this knowledge and these *words* and turn them into actions. My hair is always combed; my boots are always tied, and my appearance is always in check. I work out weekly using a very regimented routine. My room is orderly, hospital corners are a must, shirts are folded and color-coded. I know where I need to be, am never late, and do as I am told without question (for the most part). For this, I owe Coach Harrison a great deal of respect and love. I follow the *Bible*, and when I find someone in need of spiritual guidance, I listen to him/her carefully, and think of a way of helping. I constantly push myself, strive to be better, and am always looking for something that is bigger than me (whether it be God, writing, or helping others through the use of clinical psychology). I spent countless hours re-reading text books, struggling with statistical software and preparing for tests, all the while knowing my counterparts were spending half as much time on these tasks. I am very skeptical, always searching for truth, and try never to be fooled by the quick-and-easy ways in life. I am trying to be what God wants me to be as a man.

When most of us hear the word meditation, we picture a monk sitting on the ground, arms and legs crossed, with specific breathing patterns, and more times than not, chanting something odd. However, I have been taught throughout my life to meditate through *prayer*. Whether it was on the bus ride to a big soccer game in high school, sitting in the windowless rooms of the psychology department before a final, or at night, as I fall asleep, I have learned how to calm myself and stay focused through meditation. This silent communication with God is the ultimate character builder for me. Each day, I find myself becoming better at prayer. Yes, *you* can be good at prayer! I believe that by communicating with God, asking for His guidance, forgiveness, knowledge, strength, and grace, I can continue to be shaped in His image. It is through prayer that God helps me institute what I am powerless to do on my own.

It is time to confront the issue of the power of our hearts versus the power of our minds. In *The G.O.D. Experiments*, Gary E. Schwartz states,

> Just as our minds have the potential to explore all things, our hearts have the potential to love all things ... The evidence is overwhelming that our ability to love matches our ability to think. There are 'heart geniuses' as there are 'mind geniuses' (termed emotional and mental intelligence, respectively).[7]

In today's world, many young boys are gearing themselves toward becoming mind geniuses and by making this choice, they are also deciding that becoming heart geniuses is not as important.

In life, there are many great leaders who are "mind geniuses," but they lack any form of "heart genius." These men and women are extremely intelligent, can organize extraordinarily well, think quickly, outsmart their counterparts and get the job done quickly and accurately. However, these leaders are lacking a character trait that I believe is critical: the heart genius – or *love*. When marching into battle, a commander needs to know the battlefield, plan and coordinate a precise attack, and make sure that all of his men are exactly where they need to be. Without love, this man cannot connect with his troops; consequently, he will lose respect, which will ultimately defeat him and his men. A commander (leader, teacher, friend, etc.) needs to have love in order to bring out the best in himself and in others. Without love, he will lead a dark, unfulfilling life, without a purpose. A man who cannot love, or who has no "heart genius," essentially lives a meaningless life.

If I was stuck in a corner, and allowed to pick only one path, I would repeatedly choose to take the trail that leads to "heart genius." In a world dominated by sin, a man needs to discover God's love and accept it in order to get through the struggles of life and overcome the consequences of his sins and the sins of others. Our acceptance of God's love creates the meaningful life we all crave. God put us on this earth with a "life wish"; His intention is that we should live life with a purpose; we should

7 Gary E. Schwartz, *The G.O.D. Experiments: How Science is Discovering God in Everything, Including Us* (New York: Atria Books, 2006), p. 217.

long for His love, *and* we should love ourselves and others. A man who cannot love God, himself, and others, is not a man; he is simply a male. This kind of love is not something that comes easily. It must be worked on every day.

Growing up, I was loved unconditionally by my parents, and through their love, I have an extremely close, loving, committed, and respectful bond with them. I believe that, too often, parents do not show their love for their children; I was one of the fortunate ones who was loved unconditionally. However, both of my parents have often reminded me that all of their love could never match the love God has for me. That concept is mind-boggling, yet so simple. This thought alone should be enough to fill any believer's heart with joy – such *love*! In spite of all of our imperfections and sins, there is still Someone out there who loves us to our very core and will never turn His back on us.

God's undying love for me is a two-way street. Simply knowing that God loves me is enough to fill my heart with such happiness that it brings an uncontrollable, goofy, beaming smile to my face, as I type this. If that simple notion is not enough, remember that this street goes two ways. I love Him right back! Love for Him (as well as my loved ones) fills my heart with such happiness because it brings a bigger meaning to my life. Rather than walking this path alone, looking out for "numero uno," I walk this path with Him, knowing that through all my hardships and suffering, He will be right there with me. His still, small voice, constantly nudging me in the right direction – toward His will and His love, and prompting me to give my love back to Him.

As I write this, I look over at my bed and see my two cats, Donald and Harry. Their purpose in this life is minimal; they don't help pay the bills; they can't pick me up if I am stranded in a snow storm, and they spend most of the day asleep on the bed, waiting to be fed. However, all it takes is a simple "purr" from one of them and my heart is instantly filled with joy. To know that these two creatures are so dependent upon me, to know that without me they would never be as happy as they are, and to know that I give their little cat-lives purpose, as their "mother" *(yes, mother – I don't think the animal kingdom has a concept of a father)*, is one of the greatest feelings of love that I have experienced. In one way, to God, I am simply a cat. My goals, aspirations, and dreams of success can be compared simplistically to that of Don or Harry chasing a string. God created us with a basic wish to "chase a string"; that is, he created us to seek what is "fun," and to pursue what we think is important and right. Maybe this means building a good reputation, learning a skill, gaining power, or even becoming famous; ultimately, He knows that chasing strings is not what is important. As "string chasers," God expects us to ultimately develop a relationship with Him. By doing this, we mature, learn what is REALLY important, and do the hard work of making His creation a better, more peaceful, loving, Godly place. There are a million ways to do this, so, for each person who finds meaning in pursuing God's agenda, the exact life pattern is different. My willy-nilly walk through this life is not the most meaningful thing in my existence. My relationship with God is what truly counts; I believe my love for Him fills His heart and mind with joy, as His love does for me.

Finally, let's discuss what we should do when we have accepted God into our hearts. As men, we understand the importance of communication. This applies to our communication with God as well. We must talk to God through prayer and take His advice by listening carefully to Him. So, can we communicate with God? If so, how?

Out of all of the questions so far, this one is the trickiest to answer. There is a lot of gray area when it comes to "communicating with God" and includes certain aspects that some Christians are not aware of. Communication with God is a very personal, emotional, and if done with your heart and soul, amazing experience. We must turn inward, by reflecting on ourselves, and upward, by looking to God for the right answer. However, when looking to God for answers, we must understand that He does not always answer immediately, dramatically, or in what we would define as an outward expression. God communicates with a "still, small voice." Instead of spending all of our time wishing, asking, praying, and complaining to God, we should focus on listening to Him. Reading and reflecting on the text messages He has for us in the *Bible* will help.

We cannot always expect a "God-given sign" in answer to all of our prayers. God will not send down a lightning bolt and open up the heavens, proving His existence. Instead, He works in much more subtle, and often mysterious ways. When we ask for patience, God does not grant us the gift of patience; rather, He gives us opportunities to *be* patient. This form of communication is often overlooked, as we are constantly seeking obvious, outward answers, rather than looking for subtle hints that God is answering our prayers.

One might suggest that there is no God when our continual prayers for a person who is suffering are not answered in the way that we picture, or if their suffering does not end or if there is no answer to the question, "Why me, God?" Again, we need to understand how God operates in order to know what is truly happening in this type of situation. First, we need to understand that the suffering of one person is but a small part of the big picture. God's plan for them might not be what they want; their suffering may be a part of a bigger plan that He has for them. Second, sin dominates this world. God allowed man the choice to sin; as a result, man sins, and sins a lot. We need to understand that suffering can be a result of the sin which dominates the world. Once we begin to understand these facts, we can start to communicate more *intimately* with God.

When it comes to asking God questions, along with the natural *why* questions that we ask Him, I believe that we should turn our questions inward, and ask ourselves, why. One summer my family went through a lot of hardships: My grandmother passed away, my mentor had multiple health issues, my uncle slipped into major depression, and my mother was in and out of the hospital; not to mention all the hardships my father faced trying to keep the family together and keep our spirits up. When all of this came crashing down on my family, I was slightly depressed and turned to prayer for answers. However, in my prayers, I didn't ask God, "Why?" Instead I asked myself, "What is God's will?" Through prayer, I understood that these hardships were simply part of the big picture, and through all of the pain eventually came joy. My father and I grew ten times closer as we bonded and helped each other through our pain.

Understanding *how* to communicate with God goes a long way toward helping Christians grow closer to God. Instead of looking for immediate answers in external forms, we need to take a step back and ask ourselves the following questions: Is this God's will? Do I hear that still, small voice? What can I do to answer God's call instead of asking God to answer my call? God communicates like a best friend does on a day when you are feeling down: it is sometimes more in what is *not* said, than what *is* said.

Have you ever listened to God, rather than simply talking to Him? If so, what did you expect to hear and what was actually said?

Ever since I was a young kid, my parents have taught me the importance of prayer. For as long I can remember, each morning when I woke up, each night before I went to bed, and many times throughout the day, I would pray. I would thank God for all of my blessings, my family and friends, and any accomplishments or triumphs that He had helped me to achieve. If I was in a time of trouble, before a big exam, and before every sporting event, I would ask God to guide me to victory. However, it was not until I started working at 5 Stones Sports Ministry that I started listening to Him, rather than always doing the talking. Shane, the head coach and founder of the gym, who has become a brother figure to me, taught me the importance of listening. Instead of running my gums constantly, I need to increase my ability to listen for that still, small voice. Over the years, I have learned how difficult this is, but beyond that, I have learned how God's great answers are when we are patient enough to wait for His voice.

Before I give a firsthand account of the miracles that God has shown me as I have learned to listen to Him, I would like to make a brief statement about "messages from God." I am 100% convinced that God does not send us brilliant messages, written in bold lettering that is tattooed on the walls for us to see, without any effort on our part. However, if we are patient and listen carefully and listen hard, we can hear what He has to say.

Before I went to 5 Stones, I believed that if I prayed, God would answer. The results were not always what I wanted: a poor grade on a test, a loss in a big game, numerous injuries in sports, and not being able to pull a new personal record (PR) in the weight room. I was under the assumption that God was a giant wallflower, taking in everything we say, without the need for us to ever talk back. In the summer of 2010, I felt a strong urge to join the Marine Corps Officer Program. I prayed about it and asked God for guidance. I signed all the recruiter's paperwork and reported to my appointment at the Military Entrance Processing Station (MEPS). During my long day at MEPS, I completed my Armed Services Vocational Aptitude Battery (ASVAB) test, physical - including a Pulmonary Function Test (PFT), and several other tests and screenings to determine my qualification for enlistment. I was all set to head out that summer, head shaved, body in top shape, and mentally prepared. However, night after night before bed, I "heard" God telling me not to go. I didn't hear a voice in my head; I didn't receive any outward signs or direct messages. It was a feeling I can't put into words, other than I felt His presence telling me boot camp was something I should not do.

As it turned out, that summer was the most painful time that my extended family has ever gone through, as a whole, in our history together, as a family. This was the summer that I described earlier, which culminated in my grandmother's death. All the while, my father struggled, serving as the linchpin, trying to keep our family and himself together and able to function. With my mother in the midst of her own serious health struggle, who was my father to turn to? Because I was home that summer instead of at boot camp, my father had a second-in-command, someone who was able to listen to the worst of it. At night, we would sit and talk about our day, our struggles, but most of all, have a laugh or two, purely to keep ourselves from internally combusting.

One sunny afternoon this same summer, my dad realized that his cat, Bamboo, was very sick (she was *his* cat). He loved this cat, as she was a constant reminder of the simple things in life during these rough times. She would follow him around everywhere and loved him with all of her tiny kitty heart. Then she began to rapidly lose weight. My dad took her to the vet only to find out she was terminally ill at a very young age and needed to be put down immediately. He came home upset that he had lost such a close friend and asked if I would help bury her after dinner. As we headed outdoors, it began to rain, not a little, but a driving rain with terrible winds. We took turns digging her grave. As I write this with tears in my eyes, I remember how our hearts were lifted as we worked together. We began laughing, fighting back chokes and sobs, saying to ourselves, "Could it get any worse?!" As we laughed about our struggles, it hit me: NO, it couldn't get any worse. God was telling us that after the storm will come the sun. We survived that onslaught of struggles and are now experiencing the sun. God led me to stay home that summer where I was needed most.

Throughout that time, God didn't need to outwardly tell us it would be okay. We did not need to talk ourselves in circles about what the future would be, but instead, a lighter part of a dark journey was a father and his son digging a grave for a beloved pet in a rainstorm as God told them both, they would make it, and He would be with them through it all.

Manhood Discussion - Chapter 23

1. How do you believe the media, schools, and the government treat you, as a young man with a faith system? How do you, as a father, believe these cultural institutions support or fail to support your faith?

2. What do you believe God has called you to be: emotionally, physically, intellectually, relationally, and spiritually?

3. How does the fact that God loves you unconditionally affect you? How do you feel about his clear command that you are to love others?

4. List five issues that you each want to pray and talk to God about. Spend 5-10 minutes, taking turns, praying for each other's list of issues.

5. John 3:16 states, "God loved the world so much that he gave his one and only Son. Anyone who believes in him will not die but will have eternal life." How does this *Bible* verse affect your manhood journey?

What Now?

24

In this chapter, we are ready to set sail into the unknown, deal with those males who do not live up to what a man should be, and teach about manhood, God, love, and truth to all who will listen! Here we are; we've gone through our manhood training; we have been handed our sword, shield, and armor, picked out our War Horse, established good ties with our brother-warriors, and have been battle-hardened through training. Now what? No matter how much training we are given or how many hours we devote to it, the images of the impending battlefield can still be rather intimidating. Let's face it, we're outnumbered and surrounded. If history proves anything, it's that sheer numbers can win any battle; there are negative forces around us that come crashing down on us, hoping to beat us down and eventually rule the world. These cultural forces have different values, motivations, and serve different gods.

I'm pretty certain that even the best trained, courageous, love-filled young bucks out there who are ready to be transformed into men, when looking down on the battlefield, would need a change of pants. It is hard to watch hordes of males choosing to live less fulfilling lives by fighting against doing what is right. Our prisons are filled and overflowing with individuals who have willfully chosen the wrong path. But what do we as aspiring men and future Bulls do, preparing to defend our way of life? Why is it that we cannot peek into the future, take a quick glance at what is to come, if only just for a second, so that we can see what we need to do in order to come out victorious? Most importantly, remember your battle cry, gentlemen: HOKA HEY! Make sure that every day is, in fact, a great day to die. Beyond this, we cannot say what is to come; for the future is not ours to know.

Too often, I hear people complaining about what may happen next in life; they say they are nervous, because of not knowing what a new day will bring. They do not want to live by faith. It was toward the end of my college career that I found myself in an argument with an atheist. He was confused about why I was willing to sacrifice for a God who we cannot *prove* exists. He didn't understand how I could wake up every day, ready to take on life serving a higher power that cannot be mathematically or scientifically proven. He didn't like the fact I was riding purely on faith, and ignored that he couldn't prove his position either. He asked me how I could claim not to be scared of life after death if I could not prove the final outcome. I will share my answer about my views of the afterlife with you and compare it to our angst about the epic war we, as young men, are about to enter. You and I need to do what 1 Peter 3:15 states, "But make sure in your hearts that Christ is Lord. Always be ready to give an answer to anyone who asks you about the hope you have. Be ready to give the reason for it. But do it gently and with respect."

Question: If you proved that there is "life after death," how would this change your life and the ways you are currently living your life? [8]

I discussed this question with someone else about a week prior, when most of Bloomsburg had gone home for Easter weekend. Like other students who made their way home, and planned on spending a little time with their friends, I too, was looking forward to catching up on college life with my friends and reminiscing about my high school days. I was fortunate enough to have time to see my two closest allies from high school, Gabe and Alex. It was the Friday before Easter Sunday, and we decided that we would meet at the local restaurant to spend some time together.

As most friends played catch up, talked about years past, and plans for after graduation, we took a little different route. Instead of wasting our time on useless topics, or simply sharing childhood memories, we wanted to get into the good stuff, the meaty stuff, the stuff real men talk about.

8 Dr. Joseph Tloczynski, Bloomsburg University

We ventured into a discussion about God, Jesus, spirituality and religion, and eventually, stumbled across the issue of life after death. Alex is fairly convinced that there is not life after death, and when Gabe and I would pull things from the *Bible* to try to convince him otherwise, he continued his rebuttal, saying, "Yes, that is all fine and dandy, but how can we *know* there is life after death? You two keep referring to faith, but I am asking how can we be certain that there really is an existence after we die?" The reality is that we all live by faith in terms of our perspective. The Christian viewpoint, however, expresses hope. It is centered on the negative aspects of the world and how it evolved and about how Jesus came to change it. Saint Paul states in 2 Corinthians 5:8, "We are certain about that. We would rather be away from our bodies and at home with the Lord." This makes death something that we can face and do not need to fear. Alex's question got me thinking and over the next couple of days, I started to formulate an interesting series of thoughts.

What if there really was a way of knowing, instead of just having faith? What would I do if we could prove that our souls continued on after this life? I feel as if this would change my entire way of acting and my under-standing of why I am on this earth, because choosing to have faith would be less essential. As a Christian, I was brought up with the notion of "faith": Belief that there is a God, and that through His Son, Jesus alone, I can enter Heaven. However, with this amazing gift comes uncertainty. If God granted us the ability to know, 100% without a doubt, that there was truly life after death, I believe it would change how I make choices and would still not mean anything regarding my walk with God. Adam, in the *Bible*, actually physically walked with God, and he still chose to disobey Him. Faith is a powerful thing; God made faith available to us for a reason. He wanted His followers to believe in Him, acknowledge Him, and follow Him by faith. When you take away faith and replace it with fact, or hardcore evidence, it changes the nature of your relationship with God. Instead of working on our ability to believe at deeper levels, we spend our energy trying to manipulate the facts surrounding God. God works in mysterious ways; He gives us the option of making our own choices when it comes to His existence, His grace, and His power. If we knew based on fact, not faith, that He created us, ruled this earth, and was waiting for us after death, it would turn us into zombies, walking this earth without thoughts, emotions, or free will. It would be like God putting a gun to our head and then asking us if we want to have a relationship with Him. God's essence is so powerful, as seen in the burning bush, that we would have a belief in Him without argument, if we knew Him based on fact.

Adam's ability to choose a relationship with God was a critically important gift. God granted us the power of option, choice, and mostly, of free will. Unfortunately, we misused the power of choice by foolishly believing that we could become equal in power to God. We should have remained in our role as His War Horses. To know for certain, outside of faith, that there is life after death would change the nature of our relationship with God. To understand the importance of faith and how it affects our notion of life after death, I will give an example of something less meaningful: high school sports.

When I was a senior in high school, I was co-captain of my soccer team. Before every game, I mentally prepared myself for battle, whether the opposing team was 0 and 12 or 12 and 0. I made certain that I would bring my best to the game, and that my teammates were mentally prepared as well. I would make sure that each time we stepped on the playing field, we were ready to leave it all on the field, because we never knew what the final score would be. But, what if I knew the final score ahead of time? What if, before every game, I knew what the end result would be? I would walk on the field and play, simply to get the game over with. I wouldn't put my heart and soul into every touch of the ball; I wouldn't have the drive to protect my teammates, to out-hustle my opponents and to make certain I played to the best of my abilities. I would have no reason to give it my all, because no matter what happened, the outcome would have already been established. My passion, my heart, became an important variable as it could make a difference in the outcome.

Life on this earth, like my high school soccer days, is a mystery. I do not know, for certain, what the final outcome will be. But, through faith, I can hope for and *believe* in a better life to come. Every day at practice I made sure to give it my all and to make sure my teammates were as focused as I was. Every game, I stepped on the field ready for battle, and after every game, win or lose, I knew I had given it everything. Because I didn't know the final outcome, I played the entire 90 minutes with everything I had. Because I do not know, for certain, what is to come after this life, I will be more likely to live it to the fullest. I will praise God for everything He is to me and will not take Him for granted. As Hebrews 11:1 states, "Faith is being sure of what we hope for. It is being certain of what we do not see." If science could prove what the end of life is like, my drive for giving my all would be reduced. I would walk onto the soccer field of life and would not care if I missed a pass, if I didn't score or didn't make a game-changing defensive play.

When Adam chose to sin, he introduced other uncertainties to life. Because of Adam's choices, all of us have lost the certainty that scientific proof gives us because God's holiness and our sin are incompatible. Man's relationship with God can only be explained on a faith level, and as 2 Corinthians 5:7 explains, "We live by believing, not by seeing." God is the ultimate coach and He wants us to play our hearts out for Him. The final score is unknown and the game clock is winding down. Not knowing *exactly* what will happen causes us to fight harder in hopes of winning for Him, for ourselves, and for our teammates. 1 Corinthians 15:57 states, "But let us give thanks to God! He wins the battle for us because of what our Lord Jesus Christ has done." Our victory is assured, as our faith keeps our passion in the game.

Like the game of soccer, we cannot control what will happen in the final minute of the final hour of our epic battle against the powers of darkness. Instead of fearing the unknown and cowering from it, we should embrace the unknown and accept that our faith and walk with Christ can be strengthened by living within the unknown. If we did know what would happen next, we would not be trying as hard as we are now. By faith, we know the final outcome. Men need the unknown; it is what drives them to great heights and teaches them to push past their fears and weaknesses. Let us see the unknown as a challenge, an obstacle, or an *edge* and sprint to it. Let us look at each day as another *edge* when combating the evil forces around us, climb on our War Horses and prepare to wage war for what is good in our lives. Remember, you aren't the only ones who can't scientifically prove what tomorrow will bring. Our enemy is just as clueless, because their "faith" is based on chance for their own questionable power. However, many people are scared of the unknown, and try to pretend in order to escape its potential consequences in their lives. Instead of fearing the unknown, let us use our faith in the fact that God is there to walk with us through it as a great source of comfort.

There are numerous promises from God that can encourage us when we are dealing with the unknowns in our lives. 1 Corinthians 10:13 tells us, "You are tempted in the same way all other human beings are. God is faithful. He will not let you be tempted any more than you can take. But when you are tempted, God will give you a way out so that you can stand up under it." In Psalm 23:4, we are told, "Even though I walk through the darkest valley, I will not be afraid. You are with me. …" These messages from God can give us the confidence we need to practice our faith and express it to others.

A life of using a faith in Christ as a way of getting through the unknown must begin somewhere. Where are you in your faith journey? Ephesians 2:8 states, "God's grace has saved you because of your faith in Christ. …" Adam began mankind's walk into the unknown, and we can counteract the negative effects of his choice by joining up with Christ on a walk of faith. We must accept that we need something to believe in that is outside of our ability to control God, which takes away the importance of money, status, or intelligence. It is our acceptance of the gift of Jesus' sacrifices on the cross that causes our sins to be forgiven by a very holy God. Why walk through the unknown alone anymore? Submit your will to God by praying this prayer: "God, I accept that I am sinful and imperfect and that this keeps us apart. I accept the gift and grace that you offer me as a result of your Son, Jesus Christ's death on the cross for me. Enter my life in a way that empowers me to honor you. Thank you. Amen."

Let me know if you have done this and feel free to email me at mdavis@knightsofthe21stcentury.com. Congratulations! Tell others about your decision so that you can grow in your faith!

Manhood Discussion - Chapter 24

1. Have you ever lost someone you were close to through death? Share what it has been like for you to lose someone through death. What was this person like and how much do you miss them? If you could say one thing to them right now, what would it be?

2. How does it feel to live a life where there are few guarantees? What do you believe about God? What do you believe about who Jesus is? Psalm 23:4 states, "Even though I walk through the darkest valley, I will not be afraid. …" Share a time in your life when you felt like the description in this *Bible* verse.

3. What do you and your friends talk about? What do you do for fun with them? Do you have friends who you can discuss spiritual issues with?

4. Ephesians 2:8-9 states, "God's grace has saved you because of your faith in Christ. Your salvation doesn't come from anything you do. It is God's gift. It is not based on anything you have done. No one can brag about earning it." Discuss these *Bible* verses and how they apply to the manhood journey.

The Talk

You did it! After 24 chapters of reading, discussing, laughing, and maybe even crying together as you discussed your own struggles, you have gotten this far. You have one more important step which you can choose to make a part of your continued manhood journey: reading and working through the growth concepts in *Being God's Man*. What is important, to you, as a dad, is that the responsibility for who your son becomes, transfers from you to him. As manhood is accomplished, your son takes responsibility for himself. That doesn't mean that he can do what he wants or that your guidance is no longer necessary. What it does mean is that you should be able to expect him to act like he is becoming a man. He should formulate his own life goals and the contribution he makes to family life should be man-like. He needs to express himself well, stand up for what is right, accept the consequences of his actions, understand his own faith, protect the hearts of children and women, and when he gives his word, he must be willing to stand behind them, no matter what the cost.

It is also time for you to have "the talk." This is the conversation that begins the relationship process which allows him to come one step closer to being your peer. This may be uncomfortable for both of you, and yet, experience has shown us that this is often a life-changing event. Unless you have been perfect, every male needs to hear his dad admit to his imperfections. Those of you who are sons need to stop pretending that your dad is perfect or covering up how you feel about his past leadership. You need to honestly accept what has taken place in your relationship. It is only after we accept *what is and has been* that we can move to what *should* be in a relationship. This will take away any excuses you can use to not be a man in the fullest sense. You can make a copy of the survey pages that follow or request an emailed copy by visiting knights21.com/bull.

It is suggested that each of you honestly evaluate what your dad is/was like. This is something that the average son doesn't want to think about or talk about. Those of you who are dads should evaluate the ways you have grown or regressed with regard to the parenting that you received. It is a manly act for you to do this together. After you have taken a week to reflect on your relationship and have scored the survey, find a time to talk with each other in a place where you won't be interrupted. If you are completing the survey as part of a mentor/mentee relationship, share together what your own father-son relationship history has been like.

The son should tell his father the scores that he gave to his dad on each issue and the dad should respond by sharing his self-scores honestly with his son. The father should feel free to point out when his son was too generous in the scores that he gave his dad. You should spend time reflecting on memories and specific events, both positive and negative, and the meaning of these events should be shared. Go at a pace that allows you to get through each issue thoroughly. If you need to talk again at another time, that is okay. Quality is much more important than speed. Follow Jesus Christ's example on the night He was betrayed. Jesus told God the Father that He would rather not die; Jesus wished that God had a different plan for His life (Luke 22:42). God the Father was clear and direct when He asked Jesus, His Son, to make the ultimate sacrifice so that we, as humans, could relate to Him. As father and son, you need to have this type of heart-to-heart talk with each other.

When this process is complete, the father should ask his son if he is willing to forgive him for whatever he has done that is a failure as a dad and as a man. The son needs to answer honestly regarding whether or not he is willing to forgive his father. It is important for the son to clearly express his willingness to forgive his dad for each issue, using the following words: I forgive you for _____(state each issue separately). Follow this format until all of the issues have been discussed. If the son is unwilling to forgive his dad for any of the issues, the father should acknowledge that it is his son's choice whether to forgive him for his failures as a dad. The journey to manhood is a process which should be put on hold until the son is strong enough to forgive his dad. Because the father realizes he is not perfect, he should also pro-actively tell his son that when he violates (hurts) him in the future by repeating some of the old male patterns that they have discussed during this time, his son should tell him about it when it happens.

As part of this process, the son should also ask for forgiveness for the ways that he has hurt his dad and other family members. The son should tell his dad the ways that he will act more manly in the future. Before either person ends the discussion, it is important that both men deal with the issues of the past together, which allows the young man to realize that being a man is now up to him. He can no longer use his dad or anyone else as an excuse for his immaturity." This will also set the standard for the man-to-man discussions which will make reading *Being God's Man* more productive. If you choose to go this route, this type of honest discussion will also help you deal with the life circumstances that you will face together in the future. Share your stories by emailing us at bull@knightsofthe21stcentury.com. We know that "the talk" can change your lives!

Father/Son Survey

This survey will help fathers measure themselves regarding the ways that they have approached and integrated manhood principles and behaviors as observed by their sons. The survey will help sons assess their perceptions of their fathers in relation to the manhood they have modeled; it also provides a process which can heal the wounds which can be a part of relationships. It can serve as a forum for sharing memories, thoughts and feelings, which is one of the first steps toward building a strong relationship.

Often, a parent and a child may have very different memories or perceptions of a shared event from the past. This exercise will add clarity to events from the past which will increase the understanding that fathers and sons have of each other. You can make a copy of the survey pages that follow or request an emailed copy by visiting knights21.com/bull.

Instructions

- Fathers and sons should each complete the survey separately.
- Fathers should score themselves on each question, according to the rating scale below.
- Each son should score his dad according to the rating scale below.
- Fathers and sons should talk together about their answers to each question.
- Fathers and sons should identify the areas where their answers are similar and the areas where their answers are different.

1 = In this attribute/quality Dad is more similar to the characteristics of a *male.*

5 = In this attribute/quality Dad is more similar to the characteristics of a *Bull Elephant.*

1. Does Dad take care of himself physically? _____
2. How well does Dad control his anger? _____
3. How well does Dad guide his sexuality? _____
4. How responsible is Dad and is he willing to face life? _____
5. Does Dad give of himself? _____

6. Does Dad have strong relationships with other men? _____

7. Does Dad maintain a balance between work and positive pleasure? _____

8. Does Dad face the pain of life directly? _____

9. Does Dad have and hold to a high moral code? _____

10. Does Dad protect every member of his family? _____

11. Is Dad good at listening, communicating, and showing that he values others? _____

12. Is Dad able to express himself emotionally in a healthy way? _____

13. Does Dad handle decision-making well? _____

14. Does Dad inspire me to have my own faith system? _____

15. Is Dad aware of his dark side (weaknesses, failures, shortcomings, tendency toward negativity, or taking the easy path)? _____

16. Does Dad do what is required to correct his mistakes? _____

17. Does Dad forgive others when they hurt him? _____

18. Does Dad choose his life principles well and live by them? _____

19. Does Dad learn from his past and reflect healthy growth, as a man? _____

20. Does Dad act confidently, without unnecessary defensiveness? _____

21. Do Dad and I spend time together that is focused positively? _____

22. Does Dad let me know often that he loves me? _____

23. Does Dad demonstrate how to care for a woman by how he treats my mom? _____

24. Does Dad live a life of integrity and good character? _____

25. Does Dad discipline me fairly and control his anger while doing so? _____

26. Does Dad listen to me and compliment me? _____

27. When/If Dad drinks, does he drink appropriately? _____

28. Does Dad teach me how to do things and encourage me to learn? _____

29. Does Dad sacrifice himself for others and lead the family well? _____

30. Does Dad have a strong relationship with God? _____

The Bull Team

Author: Mitchell P. Davis - graduated from Bloomsburg University. Mitch comes from a rich heritage of veteran missionaries. Both sets of grandparents spent their careers in Asia with the Christian and Missionary Alliance. As a constant reminder, his middle name, Paul, is the first name of both of his grandfathers. Mitch's parents met as missionary kids in boarding school. Throughout his childhood, he has experienced not only the food of southeast Asia, but many travelers coming through his home from all over the world sharing stories, food, music and memories. Mitchell was raised in the Lancaster Evangelical Free Church and attended Eastern Lebanon County public schools before embarking on his higher education. He developed lasting friendships throughout his education at ELCO and Bloomsburg.

Mitch is an only child and comes from a small, but tight-knit, extended family. He experienced excellent loving adult interactions from the time he could communicate and is thankful to all for their investment in his growth and development. He is beyond grateful for the constant prayers of his grandmothers, Grandma Phyl (now with God), and Dot Dot (still on her exercise bike praying every morning). Mitch is thankful for his parents who raised him with their full attention and unconditional love. Both work in the social services field, which may have contributed to their consistent encouragement for him to communicate his thoughts, feelings and beliefs from the time he learned to talk. Mitch enjoys reading, pushing himself in self-discipline, and has developed a passion for writing.

Mitch would like to thank his team of close friends:

Alex Wolfe and Gabe Wertz - Thanks for all the deep and meaningful conversations throughout the years. You were two guys who I could count on while growing up.

Blake Harris - Thanks for being there, by my side, in middle school, high school, and college. Your quiet presence has always been grounding. We walked at high school graduation side-by-side and again four years later at Bloomsburg.

Sean Duffy - If it weren't for you, my senior year of college would've been much harder than it was. Thanks for always being there, no matter what my request was. I'll never forget our days down by the river or late at night, studying. But most importantly, I will never forget your unwavering trust.

Jack Risser - You know my best qualities, and you know my worst. Thanks for always having a listening ear and more importantly, thanks for holding me to high standards and keeping me on the path of manhood.

Jamie Severini - Since I've known you, I cannot think of a time you were not there for me. You placed me first and never asked for anything in return. You were my copilot through the last two years of college. If it were not for you and your unwavering friendship, my ship might have hit some damaging icebergs.

I'm happy God put you all in my life. I love you all as brothers and look forward to the adventures yet to come. You all taught me how to be a better man, and I thank you for that.

Author: Dr. Roy Smith - has worked for over 30 years as a psychologist/counselor to men and their families. During this time, he has come to appreciate the manhood journey, as many men have come into the counseling environment in order to better themselves. It has often been quite clear that many men would like to do what is right for themselves and their families, if they could understand the "how" and the "why" of the changes that are necessary and are coached accordingly. The Knights of the 21st Century program/ organization has been developed to help men grow and lead effectively in an effort to positively change our culture. The program provides tools that are designed to help men begin to see the beauty of their design, develop their giftedness, and appreciate the presence of their Creator in their lives. *Bull* is a new addition to the resources that Knights of the 21st Century offers. *Bull* is written for young men with the hope that fathers will also read it along with their sons and contribute to the father-son manhood growth process in new ways. Roy hopes his contribution to this book will be as preventative as it is restorative. Knights of the 21st Century offers the following additional resources: *The Heroic Man's Journey*, a 5-year series (24 lessons per year) focused on manhood; *Initiation - Starting Your Knighthood Team*, a 6-lesson series focused on developing men into the leaders God has called them to be; *Fighting For Your Manhood*, an 8-lesson series focused on fully understanding who you are as a man, the special mission that God has called you to participate in, and the impact on the world that you are expected to make; *Being God's Man* explores what it means to be God's man and to reflect Jesus Christ to others on a daily basis.

Roy's dream is to assist the Christian church to reach out in practical ways to those who have felt unaccepted. His goal is to demonstrate through this material that the *Bible's* truth, when applied to a life, will lead a person to greater heights of self-fulfillment, while pointing to the necessity of a daily God-man relationship. Roy has relied on the learning that is based on his early history with multiple church environments that were both good and bad for the creation of this material. As a minister's kid, he experienced good *Bible* teaching, as well as imperfection in the ways that those who claimed to be connected to God applied it.

Roy has a Master of Divinity degree and a Master's and Doctorate degree in Clinical Psychology, all of which have contributed to the content of this book. He is ordained through the Evangelical Church Alliance. He has dedicated over 30 years of his growth journey to active involvement in his own personal therapy experience and growth group experience. He reads continually in the area of personal/spiritual growth. As a licensed psychologist, certified addictions counselor, and a certified employee assistance professional, Roy has worked with a variety of men's issues.

Roy would describe himself as a lucky man because of his marriage to Jan, who is also a therapist, and because of her ongoing support for many of his idealistic "windmill attacks." His daughter, Kim, has taught him in many ways, while his son, Nick, in dealing with his own autism and Down Syndrome, has shown him the practical earthiness that life brings. Pennsylvania Counseling Services (PCS) was started in Roy's living room over 30 years ago; PCS has allowed him to receive helpful input from thousands of clients and therapists, as they have dealt with a full range of life issues on an ongoing basis.

His longtime special friends, Ruthie and Jon Davis, Becki and Don Hager, Barb and Dave Sabo, along with his new friends Keith and Lynn Walker, Clair Hoover, Director of Team Development and his wife, Bonnie, and Brian Martin, Director of Ministry Outreach and his wife, Christine, have encouraged this latest venture which is aimed toward helping males learn how to become men. Sherri Haldeman has typed for many hours. Her work and support has been much appreciated. Lou Picchio, MD, has been a challenging and supportive mentor for over 20 years. Nate Brosius, Mitch Davis, Mike Ernest, John Grisbacher, Matthew McBride, Alex McBride, Cody McBride, David Miller, Duane Miller, Tim Nicklas, Kerry Sabo, Derick Schoenly, Mark Walters, and Preston Schoenly give him hope for the future of manhood. He would also like to thank Rich Galutia, Justin Ashcraft, Mitch Hanna, Denny Geib, Ralph Eib, Clair Hoover, Jay Scott, Steve Sabol, Steve Muller, Floyd Soule, Jim Whiteman, and Bill Zeamer, from the Lives Changed by Christ (LCBC) Men's Ministry Leadership Team, for their dedication and support of Knights of the 21st Century.

Roy has had the privilege of sitting under many pastors who have taught, led, and provided good examples of what the church should be, including Chuck Swindoll, formerly of First Evangelical Free Church of Fullerton, Dave Martin, formerly of Evangelical Free Church of Hershey, and his present pastors, Pastor Jim Whiteman and Senior Pastor David Ashcraft of Lives Changed By Christ Church, who have all taught the *Bible* and its application well. Last, but not least, is Pastor Stephen Sabol, who offers a daily dose of free encouragement and wisdom through his "Thought for the Day" emails. To sign up, visit our website at knightsofthe21stcentury.com.

Editor: Barb Sabo - is a longtime friend and co-worker of Roy Smith's, who has worked in various capacities with Pennsylvania Counseling Services for over 20 years. Her gradually evolving role as an editor of the Knights of the 21st Century program materials had its beginnings on her front porch with a "pink pen" in hand. She does not attend Knights, but perhaps lends a subtle female perspective, at times, to the material without the intention to do so.

The men in her life are at various points of what this program defines as the journey to "knighthood." Her father would, at unpredictable times, respond relationally as a knight. Within the last few years, her brother has begun the long and very difficult journey towards knighthood, a journey for which he has had few role models, but is pursuing in earnest on a daily basis.

Her husband, Dave, has quite naturally and sometimes effortlessly, it seems, become the knight to her that few men with whom she has relationships have been. Her son, Kerry, has the natural tenderness that women hope for from the knights in their lives, and he is gradually learning about the differences between males and men. The editing skills that are a "part of her being" belong to her mom … and it is with love and hope that these skills are shared with all of the men who hope and aim to become knights.

Copy Editor: Laura Cramer - is a sophomore at University of Pittsburgh, studying neuroscience.

Copy Editor: Trisha Hocker - graduated from Lebanon Valley College with a Bachelor's degree in Business Administration/Management.

When you've finished reading Bull, please visit knights21.com/bull and use the following code in order to receive additional manhood resources and to have a copy of the Father/Son Survey emailed to you for your personal use.
Code: BULLSURVEY

GUESS WHAT?

The patterns that you have established by meeting with each other regularly must b
continued through joint activities with other men. The teamwork that is enjoyed wit
other men through participation in team sports or other clubs and organizations, or a
part of a class or ministry within the church, needs to be an ongoing part of your lif
The predators of life attack when we are alone. You need to have relationships wit
other men; they will challenge you, and provide support, encouragement, an
confrontation. Do not allow yourself to become isolated or lose your focus on what i
important in life. Create a manhood that you can rely on throughout your life. Chec
out the resources that Knights of the 21st Century offers to help you, and the men wh
are part of your life, continue the conversations about what really matter

FIGHTING FOR YOUR MANHOOD

This 8-lesson program, presented by five different
speakers (including Robert Amaya and T.C. Stallings of the
movie, Courageous), is designed to challenge men in the
church to develop a stonger faith in God.

KNIGHTS OF THE 21ST CENTURY
BEING GOD'S HERO IN TODAY'S WORLD

Knights of the 21st Century encourages men to become what God has called them to be. The postive approach of this program teaches men to recognize their God-given design; it also helps them discover their unique potential, and prepares them to succeed within their marital, family, work, church and community environments. Knights of the 21st Century and The Heroic Man's Journey curriculum is making an impact. Participation continues to grow! 99% of the churches that purchase the first year of the curriculum go on to purchase the second year, along with additional workbooks.

Through the unique use of the knighthood metaphor and the introduction of a new language which calls men to nobility in their thinking and actions, it motivates and challenges men to achieve their potential in all areas of life.

The first year of The Heroic Man's Journey curriculum includes:

- 24 studio-quality DVD lessons with interactive options
- 1 workbook
- Leadership CD which includes resources to help your group succeed
- Small Group Leader's Guide with 10 participant brochures

The Heroic Man's Journey curriculum can be used as a guide for weekly men's gatherings in church, prison, community center or business settings.

Contact Information
Knights21.com • pacounseling.com
1-800-777-0305
E-Mail: info@knights21.com

Knights of the 21st Century
200 North 7th Street
Lebanon, PA 17046

Published by Pennsylvania Counseling Services, Inc.

ADDITIONAL KNIGHTS OF THE 21ST CENTURY PRODUCTS

For more products, visit our website store at Knights21.com.

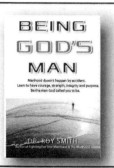

BEING GOD'S MAN

This book explores what it means to be God's man and to reflect Jesus Christ to others on a daily basis. A man's ability to reflect Jesus to others requires him to integrate God into all of who he is.

MANHOOD JOURNEY

A man is designed for a special Godly purpose, for which God has given him great potential. Knights of the 21st Century, a men's ministry curriculum used by churches around the world, is based on the material in this book, and serves as the foundation for many of the Knights resource materials.

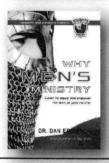

WHY MEN'S MINISTRY

A strong men's ministry is foundational to the church's fulfillment of God's great purpose for the world. This book discusses the issues that are important to an effective men's ministry program and empowers leaders to provide the kind of program that changes men's lives.

BREAKFAST DVD SERIES

Each 30-minute session challenges men to fullfill God's purpose for their lives and encourages men to be more like the ultimate man, Jesus Christ.